W9-BHO-304

DIY HOME REPAIRS

100

FIX-IT-YOURSELF PROJECTS

"To my father, Richard, for inspiring me in all the things that ended up with me writing this book. Thank you for being great."

Publishing Director: Jane O'Shea
Creative Director: Helen Lewis
Editor and Project Manager: Charlotte Coleman-Smith
Design and Art Direction: Dave Brown, Apeinc.co.uk
Research: Jenny Jacoby
Production Director: Vincent Smith
Production Controller: Leonie Kellman

Illustrators
Technical: Roy Cooper and Ian Moores
Individual tools and toolbox: Sister Arrow
Endpapers, jacket wallpaper, and section headers: Rob Hunter

Published in the United States by Adams Media, a division of F+W Media, Inc.
57 Littlefield Street, Avon, MA 02322. USA.
www.adamsmedia.com

First published in 2014 by
Quadrille Publishing Limited
www.quadrille.co.uk

ISBN 13: 978-1-4405-8529-6

ISBN 10: 1-4405-8529-6

Printed in China

Every effort has been made to ensure that all information is accurate. However, a book of this nature cannot replace specialist advice in certain cases and therefore no responsibility can be accepted by the publisher or author for any loss or damage caused by reliance upon the accuracy of such information. Bear in mind, especially if you live outside Britain, that your local conditions may mean that some of this information is not appropriate. If in doubt, always consult a qualified professional.

DIY HOME REPAIRS

100

FIX-IT-YOURSELF
PROJECTS

SARAH BEENY

WITH ANGELA F. ROBINSON

Adamsmedia

Avon, Massachusetts

CONTENTS

INTRODUCTION

Being successful at DIY is all about three things: knowledge, experience, and a good helping of determination.

Once you have the knowledge you can gather experience. Then, with a little determination, you'll soon find that you're able to take charge of maintaining and improving your own home, perhaps even saving yourself thousands of dollars along the way.

I was lucky. My father encouraged us from a very early age to do it ourselves. He was not only a very positive role model, but also expected us to pitch in. He generally had one project or another going on at home, whether it was building a new workshop or reroofing an old one. First thing in the morning during vacations and weekends, he'd come into our bedrooms and strongly suggest we get up and lend a hand: generally by removing our blankets and opening the windows!

My father always encouraged us to give things a try. In fact, when I was about thirteen he gave me a $350 budget to redecorate my bedroom. He took me to choose wallpaper, paint, and fabric, then explained how to do it and left me to get on with it. I'm not sure it was the best job in the world, but it gave me a massive amount of confidence and certainly taught me how to make curtains and hang wallpaper!

It was when I bought my first apartment with my brother, Diccon, and Graham (now my husband) that I really needed to learn fast, however. My father gave us his old drill and a few screwdrivers but the apartment had an outside toilet, no bathroom, and no kitchen; it was an enormous challenge. I think when you're young, though, you have so much more energy, and it's amazing how quickly you learn how to do things when you have to —especially, in my case, with a drip-feed of advice from my endlessly supportive father.

When I look back at those early days of DIY, I know that, with or without my father, there was one thing that really would have helped me: a plain-talking reference book that simply spelled out the most direct way of doing the jobs you're most likely to want to do. I hope that *DIY Home Repairs* is that book.

I didn't have such a book then. I remember not soaking the wallpaper long enough and ending up with bubbles. It was my father who suggested injecting them with wallpaper paste; it worked like a charm. It was he who suggested adding dishwashing liquid to the stucco to make it stay on the wall. Sadly, he didn't remind me to check where the water pipes were before nailing the floorboards down— but that's another story!

I've now had twenty years of experience working in house renovation and construction work. I've learned a lot. Now I'd love to share all the information I've gathered along the way. I'd like to demystify those projects you may keep putting off because they feel too intimidating. Above all, I want to help you gain or regain confidence in your DIY skills.

I've laid out every project in this book in simple-to-follow steps, with clear advice on how to get everything ready before you start. I've also included some of my own insider tips on getting a great finish (*How to Nail It!*) with each job.

As you'll soon see, I can't emphasize enough the importance of preparation. In fact, preparation really should take up a good 80 percent of all the time you spend doing DIY. Think, think, think again, then plan, plan, plan again— then *do*.

In the same way that you'd get all your ingredients ready before starting to cook, you should also lay out all your tools for the job, checking that you have the right equipment and essential component parts to complete it. There is nothing more annoying than getting halfway through a project and finding out there's a screw missing, or that you've chosen the wrong drill bit. That's also why I decided to have a toolbox section in this book. If you make sure you keep all the essentials (*illustrated on pages 10–11*) in your toolbox, you'll have a much more enjoyable and productive experience next time you decide to DIY.

As you build confidence, you will no doubt find your own way of approaching certain jobs. Hopefully, however, the jobs in this book—some of them basic, many requiring a little more skill and patience—will give you a firm foundation, and a great starting point. With the knowledge you'll gain, you should never again feel that you don't know where to begin.

Whether you become a full-time DIY nut or just a DIY dabbler, what's certain is that you'll have found a money-saving and creative hobby that you can enjoy for the rest of your life. It's also one that can give you far more satisfaction than you ever imagined.

Good luck!

Sarah Beeny

BACK TO BASICS

EVERYTHING YOU NEED TO GET THE JOB DONE

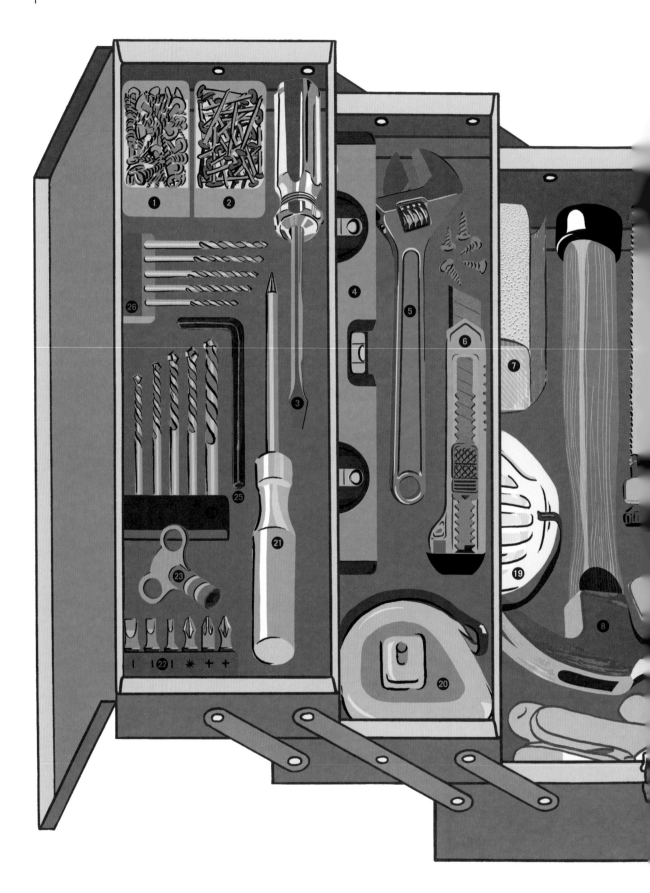

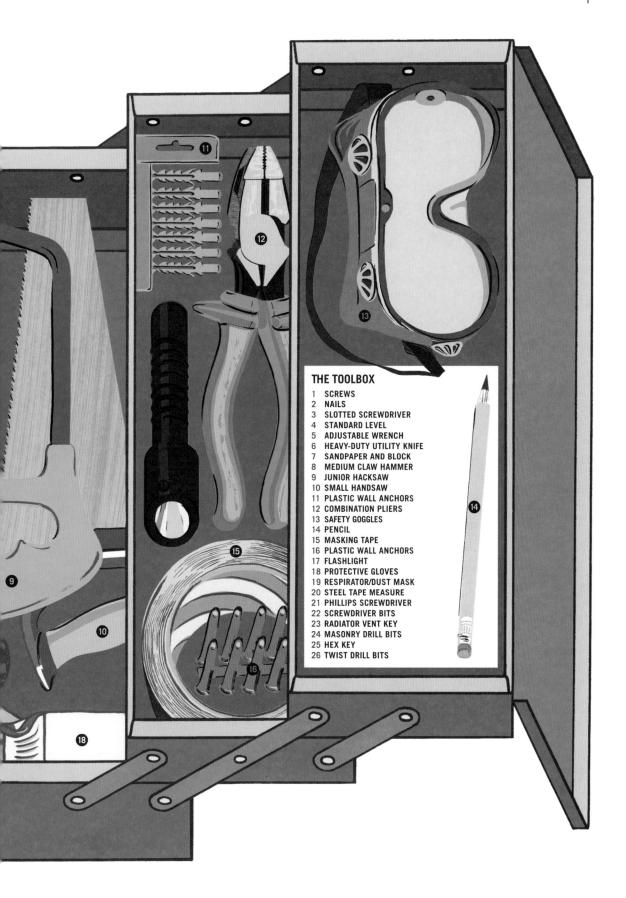

THE TOOLBOX

1 SCREWS
2 NAILS
3 SLOTTED SCREWDRIVER
4 STANDARD LEVEL
5 ADJUSTABLE WRENCH
6 HEAVY-DUTY UTILITY KNIFE
7 SANDPAPER AND BLOCK
8 MEDIUM CLAW HAMMER
9 JUNIOR HACKSAW
10 SMALL HANDSAW
11 PLASTIC WALL ANCHORS
12 COMBINATION PLIERS
13 SAFETY GOGGLES
14 PENCIL
15 MASKING TAPE
16 PLASTIC WALL ANCHORS
17 FLASHLIGHT
18 PROTECTIVE GLOVES
19 RESPIRATOR/DUST MASK
20 STEEL TAPE MEASURE
21 PHILLIPS SCREWDRIVER
22 SCREWDRIVER BITS
23 RADIATOR VENT KEY
24 MASONRY DRILL BITS
25 HEX KEY
26 TWIST DRILL BITS

THE TOOLBOX

This should have plenty of compartments so that you can get to everything easily. Don't skimp and buy a small toolbox; you will always be adding to your tool collection. Choose one that's strong enough to withstand knocks and bumps. It should have a robust handle; the weight of all those tools can be considerable.

Make sure your toolbox has:

- A LARGE SPACE FOR LONG ITEMS, SUCH AS A HAMMER AND HACKSAW
- SMALL STORAGE AREAS FOR NAILS, SCREWS, AND DRILL BITS
- ENOUGH SPACE TO KEEP SHARP TOOLS SEPARATE

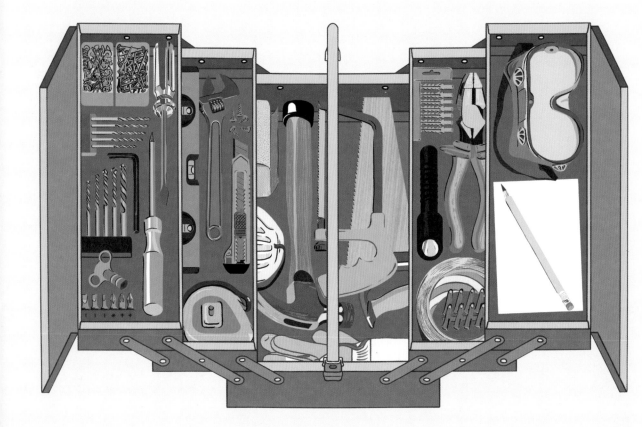

TOOLBOX ESSENTIALS

If you arm yourself with these key tools, you'll be ready for a wide range of basic DIY jobs. Good-quality tools last a lifetime.

- **SCREWS:** Multipurpose wood screws, in a range of sizes. See also page 20.

- **NAILS:** A range of sizes for inside and outside. See also page 21.

- **SCREWDRIVERS:** Slotted and Phillips, to match screws. See also page 19.

- **STANDARD LEVEL:** For checking true horizontal or vertical lines.

- **ADJUSTABLE WRENCH:** For loosening or tightening nuts and bolts.

- **UTILITY KNIFE:** A heavy-duty one can cut through multiple materials with precision. Keep a set of spare blades. Retractable types are the safest.

- **SANDPAPER AND BLOCK:** Coarse-, medium-, and fine-grade paper wraps around block and is held in place with fingers. See also page 23.

- **MEDIUM CLAW HAMMER:** For hammering in and taking out nails.

- **JUNIOR HACKSAW:** For cutting small pieces of metal, rigid plastic, and wood. Has changeable blades. See also page 22.

- **SMALL HANDSAW:** For cutting wood. See also page 22.

- **PLASTIC WALL ANCHORS:** Give screws a fixing into masonry and hollow walls. In range of sizes and types. See also page 19.

- **COMBINATION PLIERS:** For gripping, twisting, and wire-cutting.

- **SAFETY GOGGLES OR GLASSES:** To protect eyes from dust and flying debris.

- **PENCIL:** For marking measurements.

- **MASKING TAPE:** Essential for protecting surfaces when decorating. Great for marking and temporarily holding things in place.

- **FLASHLIGHT:** For working in dark corners or without light or electricity.

- **PROTECTIVE GLOVES:** Disposable rubber gloves for handling liquids, or reinforced gloves for work that's hard on your hands.

- **RESPIRATOR OR DUST MASK:** To prevent inhalation of dust.

- **STEEL TAPE MEASURE:** Retractable and robust.

- **HEX KEYS:** For assembling RTA furniture and tightening hex bolts (with six sides).

- **POWER DRILL:** For drilling into different materials and using as a screwdriver. Cordless or plug-in. Store in separate box and keep close to toolbox. See also page 18.

- **DRILL BITS:** Store a selection with your drill, including twist and masonry, for a variety of materials and hole sizes, and a selection of screwdriver bits. See also page 18.

OTHER REALLY USEFUL STUFF

- **AWL/PUNCH:** To make indentation marks for screws. A thin nail will also work.

- **CHISEL:** Use carefully with hammer or mallet to cut out notches from wood.

- **MITER BOX:** Simple device for cutting 45-degree and 90-degree miters. Use with back saw.

- **BACK SAW:** For fine woodworking and cutting miters.

- **JIGSAW:** Power tool for cutting difficult holes out of wood or cutting in restricted spaces.

- **KEYHOLE SAW:** For cutting curves and enlarging holes in wood.

- **NAIL PUNCH:** For "punching" nails flush with, or below, a surface.

- **WRENCH SET:** A set of wrenches in fixed sizes can work more reliably than an adjustable wrench.

- **DUCT TAPE:** Heavy-duty, cloth-backed tape for protecting or securing surfaces. Use only heat-resistant tape around heating and ventilation pipes.

- **GAFFER'S TAPE:** Like duct tape, but designed not to leave a sticky residue.

- **STAPLE GUN:** Very useful for creating simple upholstery.

- **STRAIGHTEDGE:** A long metal ruler for aligning and marking.

- **CHALK LINE:** For marking long, straight lines on most surfaces.

- **VOLTAGE/METAL/WOOD DETECTOR:** Indicates if any electricity cables, metal pipes, or wooden studs are hidden behind the surface where you intend to drill. It's a good idea to use a detector before drilling.

- **SPECIALTY OR PAINTER'S CAULK:** A flexible filler for smoothing over small holes, gaps, and imperfections.

- **SILICONE BATHROOM CAULK:** A flexible and waterproof sealant for use around sinks, baths, and shower cubicles.

- **CAULK GUN:** Caulk/sealant canisters slot inside for easy application.

- **PAINTBRUSHES:** Good-quality bristle brushes are the best, but decent synthetic bristles can also provide a good finish. The cheaper the paintbrush, the more bristles it will lose.

- **PAINT ROLLER AND TRAY:** Painting with a roller gives a quicker, more even finish over walls and ceilings.

- **DRYWALL JOINT KNIFE, AND PUTTY KNIFE:** Useful for applying and smoothing drywall tape, putty, and filler.

- **SPRAY LUBRICANT, SUCH AS WD-40:** Useful for loosening stiff door hinges and locks; anti-rust.

- **WORKBENCH:** A secure surface for working on so you don't damage household furniture. Portable workbenches can be folded away: useful if you're working in different areas around the house.

- **RADIATOR VENT KEY:** For bleeding hot-water or steam radiators in order to keep an old-fashioned heating system efficient.

BEFORE YOU START

CHECK YOUR TOOLS

Having the right tools is the first step to completing a job to be proud of. Don't ruin your hard work with a bad paint job because you didn't have the right type of brush, or with crooked tiling because you didn't have the right spacers. Make sure you have all the items you need. See *Tools and Techniques* (page 18).

PREPARATION

It can be very tempting to rush into a project, but time spent on preparation is essential. Each of the jobs described in this book gives clear details of any preparation needed in the *Getting Started* section. Think of each job as consisting of three stages: preparation, the main job, and finishing. Without proper preparation, your work will be harder to do, won't look as good, and it may not be as long-lasting.

MEASURE

Cutting timber, tiles, drywall, or other hardware is final, and drilling holes in the wrong place can ruin a project, so always measure twice and measure right. Correcting errors will take up more time than any that's saved by not checking your measurements.

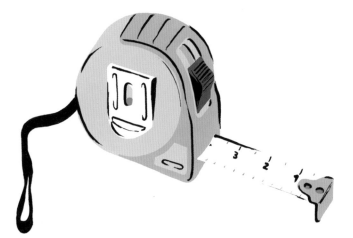

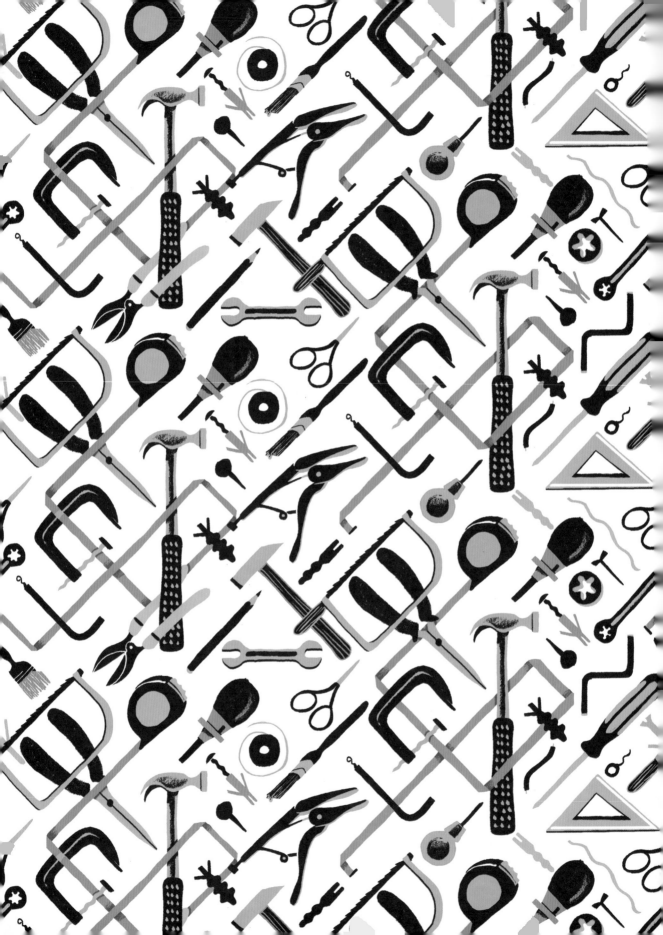

TOOLS AND TECHNIQUES

Before you buy any new tools, it's important to do a little research to make sure you buy the most suitable ones for your project. Once you have them safely home, take some time to think about techniques and read any instructions carefully.

POWER DRILLS

DRILL TYPES

- **Cordless:** Easier to use where there is no electricity, but can lack power.
- **Battery-powered:** 12–18 volt should be enough for basic jobs. The stronger the battery, the faster and more powerful the drill action.
- **Electric:** Much more powerful but will need extension cord(s).

DRILL FEATURES

- **Hammer action:** For masonry drilling.
- **Speeds:** Having variable speeds enables better control when drilling.
- **Reverse gears:** For removing screws.

DRILL BIT TYPES

Use the right bit for the material or wall type and size of hole required. Pointed ends give greater accuracy than flat ends. The most common types are:

- **Traditional twist:** In range of sizes from $5/64$–$1/2$ inch; for wood, metal, and plastic.
- **Masonry:** Hardened bits to drill into cement, concrete, or brick with hammer action.
- **Screwdriver:** For using the drill as a screwdriver.
- **Countersink:** For drilling a small recess in wood to allow flat head of screw to sit flush with or below surface of wood.
- **Ceramic tile and glass:** Sharp and curved, to cut through tile and glass safely.
- **Spade or paddle/auger bits:** For holes in wood larger than $1/4$ inch and up to $1\frac{1}{2}$ inches.

HOLE TYPES

- **Pilot hole:** Either a small hole that ensures screws go in easily and are positioned correctly, or a guide hole smaller than the size required that you then expand when drilling the final hole.
- **Countersink:** A wide, shallow hole drilled into the pilot hole, big enough so that the screw head sits just below the surface. It can then be filled and the screw head hidden. You can buy a special countersink bit, or just use a large bit, big enough to make a dip.

DRILL SAFETY

As a rule, it's a good idea to wear safety glasses or goggles when drilling; dust particles or chips can fly into your eyes. Always use goggles when drilling into masonry or hard materials. Remember to check for pipes and cables before drilling, and be very careful when drilling above or below electrical sockets.

WALL ANCHORS

Screws will only hold in masonry walls if used with anchor plugs. As you screw into it, the plug expands to grip the sides of the hole, holding it in place.

Choose wall anchors based on the material being fastened to and weight of object being attached. Fluted plastic screw anchors for solid walls are usually color-coded, depending on the drill bit diameter. Hollow wall fasteners include jet bolts and toggle bolts, which screw directly into drywall and replace plastic anchors or plastic toggles.

FOR SOLID MASONRY

- **Plastic wall anchors:** Available in various sizes to hold various weights. Lightly tap into drilled hole, then drive in screw to secure.
- **Hammer-in wall toggles:** Hammer to insert wall anchor into drilled hole, then fix with pre-supplied screw or nail.
- **Self-tapping concrete screws:** Drill directly into concrete; no pilot holes required.

FOR DRYWALL/HARDBOARD/HOLLOW WALL

- **Plastic wall anchors:** Come with small wings that open up on the other side of the cavity to hold screw in place. These can be light- to medium-duty.
- **Drywall screws:** Screw straight into the drywall with no pre-drilling required.
- **Heavy-duty metal hollow wall toggle bolts:** Umbrella or wing fixings open up on the other side of the cavity to disperse weight and hold screw in place. Can be unscrewed but the fastener will be lost in the cavity.

CHOOSING THE RIGHT ANCHOR FOR YOUR OBJECT

- Use lightweight fasteners for items such as curtain rods, tiebacks, pictures, and small mirrors.
- Use medium-weight fasteners for bathroom accessories, lightweight shelves, pictures, mirrors, wall lights, and cabinets.
- Use heavyweight anchors for bookshelves, cupboards, shower screens, TV brackets.

SCREWS AND SCREWDRIVERS

SCREWDRIVER TYPES

Be sure that you match the screwdriver head to the screw and get a good fit, or you'll risk stripping the screw, making it impossible to remove. The main screwdriver heads are:

- **Phillips:** Fits cross-type screws.
- **Slotted/flat:** Fits single-line-type (slotted) screws.
- **Pozi-Driv®:** Fits star-type screws.

It is best to have at least one of each type of screwdriver in your toolbox, in large and small sizes. You can choose from handheld or electric, or you could opt for a power drill with screwdriver bits. Handheld screwdrivers with rubber grips are easiest to handle; electric screwdrivers can save time, but if you have a power drill, invest in some screwdriver bits to save time and effort. See *Drill Bit Types* (opposite).

SCREW SIZES

Most screws in hardware stores are in inches, but they can be labeled two ways.

- **In inches,** a screw labelled No. 8 x 2.5in, has a thickness/gauge number 8 and a length of 2.5 inches.
- **In metric,** a screw labelled 4.0 x 60mm has a thickness/gauge of 4mm and a length of 60mm.

The most useful screws to have in your toolbox are standard wood screws No. 8 and No. 10 in various lengths.

SCREW TYPES

- **Traditional wood screw:** For use in wood. Screw head will sit above wood surface unless countersink holes are drilled before screwing in.
- **Masonry screw:** Strong enough to be driven into masonry without a wall anchor, but a pilot hole is still needed.
- **Particle board screw:** For use in particle board or wood. Deep threads extend right up screw head.
- **Decking screw:** Long screws for securing decking boards.
- **MDF screw:** For securing MDF.
- **Raised-head woodscrew:** Good alternative to multipurpose screw, if you don't mind screw head being visible.
- **Mirror wood screw:** Sits above wood surface. More decorative, for when you want screw head to be a feature, or when you need access, such as to a bathtub panel
- **Drywall screw:** For fixing drywall to timber studs.
- **Modern wood screw:** Screws into soft wood without pilot hole. Has double thread.
- **Security screw:** For fastening locks and security devices. Head shape allows screw to go in, but not come out.
- **Sheet-metal screw:** For fastening metal. A sheet-metal screw cuts its own thread as it is tightened.

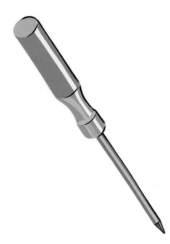

SECURING TO WOOD, INCLUDING WALL STUDS

For pilot holes, use a No. 8 screw with a $5/64$ drill bit, or a No. 10 screw with a $3/32$ drill bit. No wall anchors needed. Ensure length is appropriate for a secure fastening.

SECURING TO MASONRY

- **For light items:** Use No. 6 or No. 8 screws, with $3/16$ masonry drill bit and appropriate wall anchors.
- **For general items:** Use No. 8 or No. 10 screws, with $15/64$ masonry drill bit and appropriate wall anchors.
- **Medium to heavy items:** Use No. 10 or No. 12 screws, with $17/64$ masonry bit and appropriate wall anchors.

Minimum hole depth should be the length of the anchor used, but common sense is needed. Older walls with soft brick or thick plaster need drilling a little deeper. Choose a screw that will go through the item to be fastened and well into the plastic anchor. Remember plaster provides no grip; it is brick, cement, or concrete that provides the anchor. If the hole ends up too big, pack around the anchor with matches. See *Wall Anchors* (page 19).

HOW TO FIND A WALL STUD

Either use a handheld, battery-operated wood detector and follow manufacturer's instructions, or use the hammer-and-nail method. Tap firmly all along your wall with your knuckles and listen for a change in the sound. In areas where the wall sounds denser and more solid, try gently tapping in a thin nail in an inconspicuous area near the base of the wall. If there is resistance, you have found a stud. Most houses have studs made of 2 x 4s and positioned 16–24 inches apart.

HAMMERS

BASIC HAMMER TYPES

- **Claw hammer:** The basic hammer for all toolboxes. Remove nails with claw.
- **Pin hammer:** For hammering in fine or small nails, such as finish nails and tacks.
- **Drywall hammer:** For attaching drywall to wooden studs.
- **Lump hammer:** Big metal hammer for heavier work.
- **Ball pein/ball hammer:** For metalwork; rounded ball shapes the metal.
- **Mallet:** Made of rubber or wood. Wide area gives a soft blow. Use for tapping items gently and firmly into place. Use with chisel.

HAMMERING TECHNIQUES

A simple rule for hammering is that the smaller the hitting area of the hammer, the greater the force; the larger the area, the gentler the force.

- For accuracy, hold handle nearer the head; for greater power, hold it near the base.
- Aim to hit the target square-on, not at an angle.
- Try to use your whole arm and elbow when swinging a hammer, keeping your wrist straight. Allow the hammer to do the work, not your arm.
- Use a hard surface. Soft surfaces such as carpets will absorb some of your effort.

SAFETY AND PROTECTION

- Check that the head is firmly attached to the handle, and the handle is in good condition with no splits or splinters. If not, do not use!
- Look out behind and around you before swinging the hammer. Don't catch it on anything or anyone.
- Protect delicate surfaces (such as tiles, which can be tapped into place) by hammering gently onto thin board held on top of surface.

NAILS

BASIC NAIL TYPES

- **Round-head nail:** General-purpose nail for joining wood. May split wood if driven too far, however. **Angular ring-shank nail** has grooves for better grip.
- **Finish nail:** Smaller head fits flush with wood surface and reduces splitting.
- **Oval-head nail:** Like finish nail but oval shape further reduces splitting.
- **Roofing nail:** For attaching asphalt or roofing felt. Often galvanized to cope with weather conditions.
- **Masonry nail:** Hard, thick nail for securing wood to stone or brick.
- **Drywall nail:** For hanging drywall. Wide, flat head designed not to break drywall face.
- **Siding nails:** Long galvanized nails to attach siding or cladding to houses.

SAWS

SAW TYPES

The fewer teeth-per-inch (TPI), the coarser the cut; the greater the TPI, the smoother the cut.

- **Hacksaw/junior hacksaw:** For small metal- and wood-cutting jobs. Inexpensive.
- **Back saw:** A stiffened top edge and fine teeth, giving good control for fine woodworking. Best saw to use with miter box.
- **Hand saw:** Classic saw for cutting long pieces of wood in straight lines. Use when cut is too long for a back saw.
- **Circular saw:** A circular-bladed power saw, best suited for making long, straight cuts in wood quickly and easily.
- **Jigsaw:** A power saw best for cutting difficult holes, curves, or patterns out of wood. Small size makes jigsaws good for working in restricted space, and for finishing cuts that regular saws can't complete. Not suitable for fast, long, or straight cuts.
- **Keyhole saw:** Shape allows for cutting curves, small or awkward holes, and enlarging holes in wood.
- **Miter box:** Choose box size to fit wood. Use back saw and the guide slots to cut precise 45-degree or 90-degree angles in wood for mitered corners.

SAWING TECHNIQUES

Workbenches are the best place to do sawing work. You can clamp wood securely in place and work in a clear area where you won't damage anything. If you don't have a workbench, other surfaces can act as one. Rest the wood on top of a low surface (such as an old coffee table) with excess extending off the "bench." Use your knee and body weight to secure wood and saw along marking. Catch excess before it snaps off.

To get a clean cut

- Ensure that your blade is sharp; a dull blade will never make a perfect cut.
- Choose a blade with the right TPI grade for your needs (see above).
- Avoid letting the wood snap off before you complete the cut. Support both ends of the wood so that the end you're not holding doesn't have far to fall and won't snap off. You can balance this "free" end on scrap support wood, or ask a helper to hold it.
- If you are supporting the free section of wood, don't pull it towards you or the wood will bend in towards the saw as the cut progresses. This will pinch the saw and cause the wood and/or saw to buck, which will interrupt the clean cut.
- If possible, use a vise to clamp one end of wood, freeing your hand to control the saw.
- Start with the good side of the piece of wood face up and saw at a 45-degree angle.
- Always cut into the wood so that the blades pull into the wood from the finished/right side. Ensure that you engage the teeth on your forward stroke.
- Put masking tape on both sides of the cut's edges in order to hold wood fibers in place.

Using a jigsaw

- Choose the right blade. Use a wood-cutting blade for wood, a metal-cutting blade for metal, a laminate-cutting blade for laminate, and a ceramic-cutting blade for tiles.
- Check that your blade is sharp. Maximum cutting depth is about 2–3 inches thick, depending on blade.
- To start sawing in the middle of a piece of wood, drill a large pilot hole first.

Using a circular saw

- Set the blade depth so that the blade extends around $\frac{1}{4}$-$\frac{1}{2}$ inch at most out of the wood. Too deep and the blade will be less effective and much more dangerous. Measure the blade depth alongside edge of wood before you turn the saw on.

- Support any fall-off wood to ensure a clean cut all the way through.

- If the saw wanders from the marked cut-line, stop and start again on the right track, rather than trying to steer the saw back.

Caution: Circular saws can be very dangerous if not used as per manufacturer's instructions.

SANDPAPER

Sandpaper is graded by the number of abrasive particles per square inch. The lower the number, the coarser the grit and the rougher the finish.

SANDPAPER GRIT GRADES

- **Extra coarse/coarse** (16–50) · **Medium** (60–80) · **Fine** (100–120)
- **Very fine** (150–240) · **Extra fine** (320–360) · **Super fine/ultra** (400–1000)

Coarse, medium, and fine grades are really all you need for general DIY. You will use fine grades for finishing but coarser grades for smoothing cut ends. Coarser grades remove more material but leave a rougher finish; finer grades remove less but give a smoother finish. Sand using progressively finer grades for best results.

SANDING BY HAND

Sandpaper usually comes in 9 x 11-inch sheets. Cut them into quarters and wrap around a sanding block. Blocks are usually made of cork but you could also use a piece of wood measuring roughly $3\frac{1}{2}$ x $2\frac{1}{2}$ x 1 inch: about the size of a dishwashing sponge. Always sand with the grain—in other words, along the line of the wood.

POWER-SANDING

Some power sanders have bag attachments for collecting dust and some can even connect to your vacuum cleaner; this is a great feature, since sanding causes a huge amount of dust and if you have to do it indoors you'll be cleaning the dust from every room for weeks as it settles! Always use a dust mask/respirator when doing any type of sanding. Some particles, especially old paint, can be very nasty if you inhale them.

- **Belt sander:** Great if you want to remove a lot of material quickly. Works with a belt of sandpaper stretched over rollers, so only sands in one direction.

- **Orbital sander:** Good for achieving smooth finishes on large, flat areas, but can leave circular marks because of the way it rotates.

- **Random-orbit sander (ROS):** This is the best all-rounder, combining the speed of a belt sander with the smoothness of an orbital sander, with less risk of surface-marking.

- **Detail sander:** Shaped a little like an iron, this type of random-orbit sander is great for sanding tricky corners as well as flat surfaces. It doesn't usually come with a dust bag, so you won't want to do huge areas. Often comes palm- or hand-sized.

HOW TO USE A POWER SANDER

- Select the grade of abrasive paper you need and attach it to the sander. This can vary, depending on type, so refer to manufacturer's instructions.

- If it has a vacuum cleaner attachment or dust bag, attach this and turn it on.

- Hold the sander against the surface you want to sand and switch on.

- Keep the sander moving over the surface until you have a smooth finish.

PAINTING

PAINT

There are two types of basic paint, both of which contain volatile organic compounds, or VOCs. These are chemicals that help most paints perform as expected but are toxic to the environment. There are now eco-friendly alternatives available.

- **Oil-based:** Dries slowly, allowing brush marks to even out and giving a glossy, durable finish. Dispose of waste paint carefully to minimize environmental impact. Best for smaller areas like furniture, moldings, and outside, but banned in some parts of the country due to toxicity to the environment.

- **Water- and latex-based:** There are many different types for all surfaces. Quick-drying, easy to use, easy to clean, with less odor than oil-based.

PAINT FINISHES

- **Matte/flat:** Latex-based paint with little or no shine, so is helpful in disguising uneven surfaces because it doesn't reflect light. Not very durable and difficult to keep clean. Generally used on walls and ceilings.

- **Eggshell/satin:** Higher than matte in sheen and durability. Essentially matte with a little sheen, like real eggshells. Covers imperfections well. Better than matte in high-traffic areas. Generally used on walls and ceilings.

- **Satin:** Shiny and reflective, and can be washed, so suitable for bathrooms, kitchens, children's rooms, halls, and stairways. Can be used for trim, doors, and furniture. Doesn't cover wall imperfections very well.

- **Gloss:** High-shine, washable, and more durable than other finishes; reserve for windows, doors, and furniture. Oil-based glosses are most durable for exterior use, but are toxic and difficult to apply well.

PAINT TYPES

- **Flat acrylic latex:** Water-based, dries quickly. Two coats usually needed. Mainly used on walls and ceilings. Doesn't generally need an undercoat or primer but you do need a primer coat on new drywall. There are many types. For example: one-coat flat latex (paint and primer) is thicker, with better coverage, so you only need one coat; kitchen and bathroom paint is moisture- and grease-resistant, and washable.

- **Primer-sealer:** Always use this on new hardwood. Blocks resinous stains that would otherwise show through the paint. No need for extra primer. Shellac primer stops the bleed-through of resins.

- **Primer:** If you are using oil-based paint on unpainted wood you will need to add a coat of oil-based primer, or the paint won't stick properly. If you're using flat latex paint, the paint soaks into the wood to act as its own primer. You may need more than one coat, though.

- **Undercoat:** Some paints are formulated not to need an undercoat but you will always get a better result using one. Always use one if you are painting over dark or strong colors.

- **Topcoat:** Your final coat of paint in your desired finish.

PAINTBRUSHES

Give thorough results, but can be slower than using a roller and leave brush marks.

- **Natural fibers:** Best suited for oil-based paints and not for flat latex, as the bristles soak up the water and become limp.

- **Synthetic fibers:** Can be used for any paint type.

- **Chisel-edged brush:** Ideal for cutting-in or painting straightedges.

- **Split-end brush:** Holds more paint, and spreads paint smoothly and evenly.

The size of brush required depends on what you're painting. Small brushes (1–1½ inches) are good for intricate work; medium brushes (2 inches) for doors and baseboards; and large brushes (4–6 inches) for walls, floors, and ceilings.

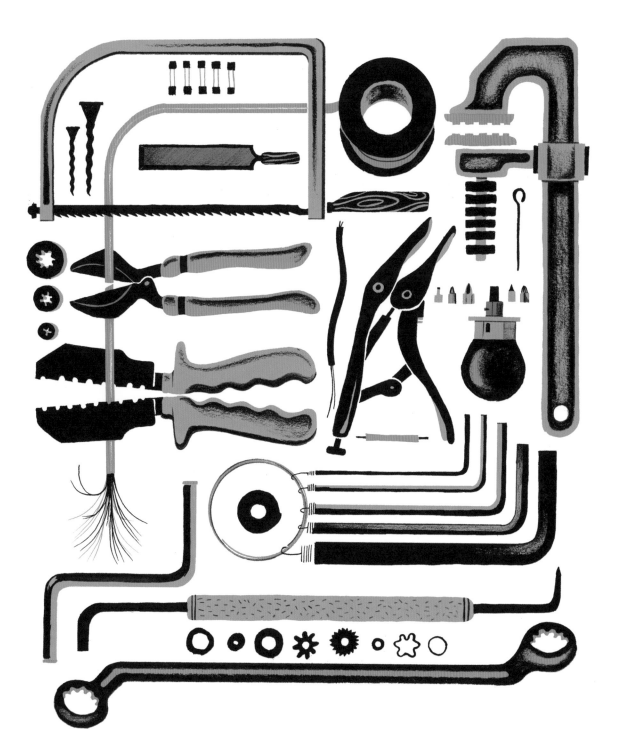

PAINT ROLLER

Covers walls quickly, but more coats needed as paint goes on thinly. Frame is made from durable wire cage with a sleeve of wool or synthetic material, which can be changed easily. Use with roller tray and pour paint into the deep end or reservoir. Dip roller into paint and run the roller over the the tray's ribbed surface to apply evenly. You'll still need to cut in around edges with a paintbrush.

- **Short-pile:** Gives smooth results. Not for rough walls.
- **Shaggy-pile:** For textured results or rough walls. Finish edges with a brush.

SPRAY PAINT

Provides a professional-looking finish and is easy to apply. Great for improving the look of old furniture, or for objects with awkward surfaces. Use thin, multiple coats. Place small objects inside a cardboard box while spraying. For larger objects, work outside if possible, or use masking tape, scrap cardboard, and drop cloths to protect surroundings.

TIPS FOR PAINTING INSIDE WALLS

- **Edges:** These blend in better if you paint them first. This is called "cutting in." Paint overlapping parallel strips perpendicular to the edge, then one long sweeping line alongside the edge.

- **Walls:** Start painting close to the light source (window), painting in bands, one at a time, as you move away from the light source.
- **Ceilings:** Paint ceilings before walls, as paint will inevitably spray.
- **Roller:** Angle roller at around 45 degrees, using even strokes in random directions. Start each freshly loaded roller in a new place, working back towards last painted place.
- **Brush:** Paint panels of one square yard at a time, blending edges in while still wet.

TIPS FOR PAINTING OUTSIDE WALLS

- Paint when the weather is fine and dry.
- Try to paint in the shade when possible; direct sunlight can make it difficult to see how paint is going on, especially with white paint.
- Complete one section at a time, using windows and drainpipes to mark boundaries.
- Start at the top of the wall and work down since paint will splash on surfaces below.
- "Stipple" the paintbrush on heavily textured walls by holding brush at 90 degrees and dabbing paint on. Vary the direction of the brush as you go.
- Protect drainpipes by taping newspaper around them. Push paintbrush carefully behind drainpipes.
- Start new brushload of paint in unpainted area and work back to last painted section.
- Paint again in opposite direction to get an even coverage.
- Paint corners and edges in same way as internal painting.

PAINTING WOOD

When choosing paint and primer for wood, you'll find that many modern paints combine stain or resin-blocker and primer (necessary for bare wood), primer and undercoat, or topcoats that require no undercoat. Water-based acrylic or latex paint is flexible and can be a great time-saver. If using oil-based paint, however, it might be best to stick to the traditional method (see opposite). Talk to the staff at your local paint or decorating store for advice.

The traditional approach is to follow three key steps:

① Primer: Seals bare wood and provides a foundation for the paint that follows. Sand lightly after priming. Paint alcohol-based shellac over new wood to seal knots and stop sap from seeping through.

② Undercoat: Main body of the paint. Provides good coverage and ensures a good bind between the topcoat and surface. Where there is a change of color, two coats may be needed. No need to sand afterwards. Choose a color that is close to your topcoat.

③ Topcoat: Is the gloss (or satin, eggshell) that provides the finishing layer. For external wood, two coats will give a longer-lasting finish. For internal wood, one coat should be adequate, unless covering a strong color. For oil paint, leave a few days between coats. If applying more than one coat, sand lightly once fully dry.

GENERAL PAINTING RULES

- Follow these key steps: clean; sand; prime; undercoat; two coats of topcoat paint. Painting wood is a combination of these steps, so select as appropriate.
- Prepare thoroughly so surfaces are clean and grease- and dust-free and other surfaces are protected.
- Buy the best paint and brushes you can afford since quality does make a difference.
- It's much better to paint two thinner coats than to try to apply too thick a coat at once. You don't want the paint to drip.
- For preparation, see individual jobs, *Painting and Decorating* (pages 142–170).

CLEANING UP PAINT

Water-based paints

- Remove excess paint from brush or roller and roller tray by squeezing or pouring back into paint can. Wipe with old cloth.
- Stir brush or roller in large bucket of warm water and dishwashing liquid. Use at least three changes of water, fanning bristles out, or massaging your fingers into the roller to work out the paint.
- Rinse brush, or roller and tray, under faucet until water runs clear; dry on old cloth.
- Store brushes bristles-up in old jars, with rubber band around bristles to keep together.

Oil-based paints

- Remove excess paint from brush by squeezing back into paint can. Wipe with old cloth.
- Wearing rubber gloves, pour mineral spirits into an old glass jar or ceramic bowl. (NB, do not pour mineral spirits into plastic.) Stir brush into the mineral spirits, working it into the bristles.
- Rub brush back and forth over your hand to rub the spirits into the bristles.
- Add dishwashing liquid to the bristles and rub in using your fingers.
- Squeeze out as much of the paint/spirits/dishwashing liquid as possible onto paper towels.
- Rinse brush under hot water, squeezing as much out as possible.
- Repeat above steps four or five times.
- Finish by rubbing in small amount of mineral spirits and dishwashing liquid and do not rinse.
- Wrap brush in paper towel, squeezing out as much moisture as possible.
- Store brushes, bristles-up, in old glass jars, with a rubber band around bristles to keep them together.

SAFETY

No matter what job you are about to tackle, safety should always be your first consideration.

WORK SPACE

- **Clear your work space:** Don't leave anything lying around that you could easily trip over when carrying a freshly pasted sheet of wallpaper, for example; or you might drip paint or dust. Make sure any cords or cables are kept well out of your way.

- **Ventilate your work space:** Be sure to have a plentiful of supply of fresh air when working with oil-based paints, paint stripper, and other chemicals. If you're creating lots of dust, open a window—but not an internal door or it will escape into the rest of your home.

- **Make sure your work space is well-lit:** Struggling to see can be tiring as well as dangerous.

CLOTHING

- **Avoid loose clothing, shoes, hair, and accessories:** Eliminate the chance of anything getting caught in your work or power tools.

- **Wear comfortable, old clothes:** Protect your body with full-length pants, long-sleeved T-shirts or sweatshirts, and tough boots. Pockets are useful for holding tools. Avoid woollen clothes that can leave fibers on your work.

- **Wear protective clothing:** Kneepads for working with flooring; rubber gloves to protect your hands from harsh liquids; reinforced gloves for anything hard or sharp on your hands; dust mask/respirator to protect your lungs from fine dust; safety goggles or glasses to save your eyes from dust and debris; earmuffs for even slightly noisy work over an extended time. Be wary of chemicals that may be toxic. Always read manufacturer's guidelines. You may need added protection or even a respirator mask in some situations.

BEST PRACTICES

- **Put away sharp tools immediately after use.**

- **Be considerate about where you set up a ladder. Make sure that anybody who is likely to be passing by is aware that you may be up a ladder.**

- **Keep a cell phone on your person in case of an accident.**

- **Don't work when you're tired.**

HOW TO USE THIS BOOK

The key features that accompany each of the jobs in this book will help you get the most out of your DIY projects. They've been designed with clarity in mind, but also with the idea that not everyone will approach each task in the same way. There are choices to make in terms of the tools you use and how thorough you want to be, which will depend on your experience, budget, and confidence. Whatever your skill level, the job can be tailored to your needs.

↑ TOOL UP
↓ TOOL DOWN

It's often possible to make use of the basic toolbox you already own, rather than buying new equipment. However, for some of the larger, or more time-intensive jobs, it really is worth investing in some specialized tools and materials—at the end of the day, you may save money as well as time. Where there is a choice, you'll see the Tool up/Tool down arrows, so you can make the decision yourself.

⚠ Look for this symbol in the tools list. It will alert you to the fact that special care is needed when using this particular tool or material and that you may need to wear protective clothing such as goggles, masks, or gloves. See *Clothing* (opposite). If in doubt, refer to manufacturer's instructions.

GETTING STARTED

Nothing is more important to DIY success than preparation. Take time to read this section, which accompanies every job in this book, big or small; don't be tempted simply to jump straight in. You'll save yourself a lot of time and hassle further down the line if you plan ahead properly.

⚠ STAY SAFE! Take extra precautions when you see this warning. The job may require you to turn off the electricity supply before starting, or it may involve handling electrical wiring or hazardous materials. If in any doubt, consult a professional.

 Whenever the step number of a job has an outline around it, you'll find an illustration to accompany it.

Reading this section will give you the edge. You'll find tips and hints on how to give your job the very best finish. This should mean your job or project will last longer but the results will be more impressive.

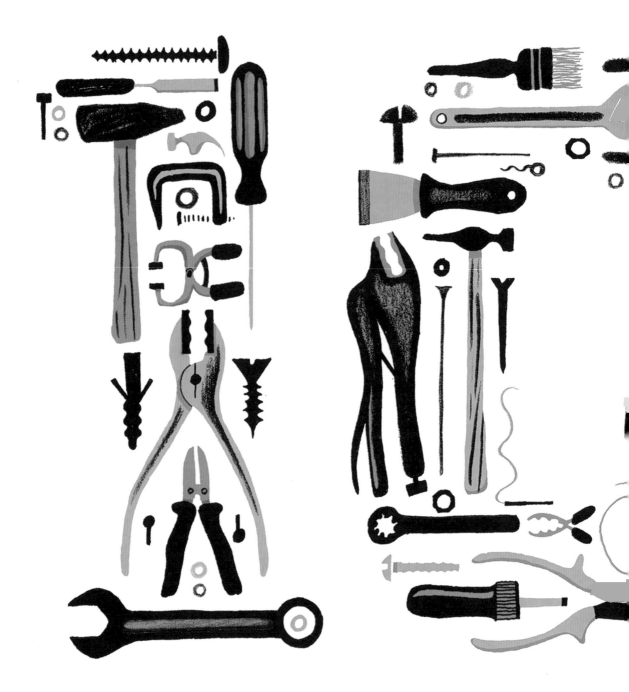

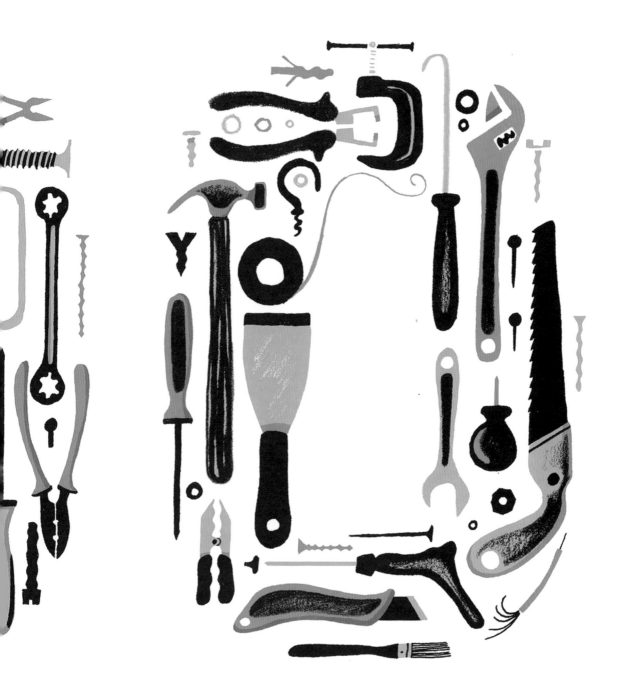

BATHROOMS
AND
KITCHENS

EVERYTHING YOU NEED TO GET THE JOB DONE

RENOVATE GROUT

01

Tiles actually rarely wear out—it's the grout that generally lets them down. Renovating grout can be a quick and cheap way to freshen up the look of your bathroom or kitchen.

YOU'LL NEED

OLD TOOTHBRUSH AND DISHWASHING LIQUID

MATERIALS FOR GROUTING (SEE PAGE 34)

PLUS, AS NEEDED:

VINEGAR AND BAKING SODA

MOLD AND MILDEW REMOVER

HOUSEHOLD BLEACH

⚠ **TOOL UP** GROUT RAKE OR REMOVAL TOOL

TOOL DOWN UTILITY KNIFE

VACUUM CLEANER WITH NARROW NOZZLE ATTACHMENT

GROUT SEALER

SILICONE KITCHEN AND BATHROOM CAULK AND CAULK GUN

GETTING STARTED

Start by cleaning the area with an old toothbrush and dishwashing liquid. If the dirt is stubborn, try a paste of vinegar and baking soda. If it's moldy, try a mold and mildew remover, or a solution of one part bleach to eight parts water. If dirt or mold persists, you will need to remove and replace the grout.

WHAT TO DO

❶ Starting at the top of a vertical joint, gently pull the grout removal tool or knife down the center of the grout line. Work to a depth of around ⅛ inch. You need enough space for new grout to take hold, but don't go too deep. Repeat along the horizontal lines. Be careful not to dislodge tiles and try not to slip and scratch the tile surface.

❷ Use an old toothbrush, or the narrow nozzle attachment on a vacuum cleaner to remove all dust and debris from the joints.

❸ If using powdered grout, mix it according to instructions. Apply grout as for *Grout Tiles* (see page 34).

❹ Apply grout sealer, and reapply waterproof silicone caulk, if needed. See *Apply Silicone Caulk* (page 46).

HOW TO NAIL IT!

• You can whiten grout by using a grout pen or reviver that will paint a white or colored finish on top of old grout.

• If you need to renovate a large section of grout, it's worth investing in a power tool.

• Never wash ANY grout down the drain because it WILL harden in the P-trap and you will have to cut out the section.

GROUT TILES

02

Grout is the waterproof cement that goes between the tiles. All tiling must be finished with grouting, and this is the really satisfying part! You can create very different looks with colored grout. For more outlandish combinations, test a small area first. Beware, though, as bold grouts are unforgiving of less than perfectly cut tiles.

▶ YOU'LL NEED

GROUT (PREMIXED OR POWDERED)

BUCKET OF WATER,
IF USING POWDERED GROUT

▲ **TOOL UP** GROUT SPREADER

▼ **TOOL DOWN**
PLASTIC KITCHEN SPATULA

DAMP SPONGE

▲ **TOOL UP** GROUT SHAPER

▼ **TOOL DOWN** YOUR FINGER

CLEAN, DRY CLOTH

GROUT SEALER, IF NEEDED

GETTING STARTED

If using powdered grout, mix it up according to the manufacturer's instructions. Always add the powder to the water instead of the other way around. Aim for a thick, creamy texture a bit like toothpaste. Check that you have enough for the job, but don't mix too much at once.

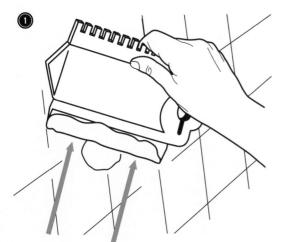

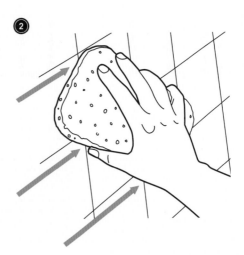

WHAT TO DO

① Use the grout spreader or spatula to spread golf-ball-sized lumps of grout over the whole tile surface in long, upwards, diagonal strokes. Hold the rubber edge of the spreader at a 45-degree angle. Work into all the joints.

② Use a damp sponge to wipe away any excess grout. Pull the sponge lightly across each right angle once. Turn it over to use the clean side, then rinse in a bucket of clean water and repeat.

③ When the grout has hardened slightly, use a grout shaper or your finger to neaten up the joints. If any gaps appear, apply more grout with your fingertip. Sponge off any excess.

④ Allow several hours (preferably overnight) for the grout to dry. Polish up the tiles with a clean, dry cloth.

⑤ Once grout is dry, apply grout sealer, if needed, according to the manufacturer's instructions.

HOW TO NAIL IT!

- Work on areas of about one square yard at a time so that the grout doesn't harden before you have finished.

- Sponge off excess without delay. It is really difficult to remove hardened grout.

- Never wash ANY grout down the drain as it WILL harden and block the P-trap and you will have to cut out the section.

CUT TILES

Tiling, especially on a flat, small, regular area, doesn't have to be tricky. It gets more complicated when you need to tile over larger spaces that have plenty of curves and obstacles, but with practice, patience, and the right tools, you'll soon be able to master the art of cutting tiles.

▶ YOU'LL NEED

RULER

CHINA MARKER

SAFETY GOGGLES OR GLASSES

PROTECTIVE GLOVES

↕ **TOOL UP** TILE CUTTER FOR STRAIGHT CUTS; JIGSAW, WITH TILE-CUTTING BLADE, PLUS CLAMP, FOR SHAPED CUTS

↕ **TOOL DOWN** TILE-SCORING KNIFE FOR STRAIGHT CUTS; TILE SAW AND CLAMP, OR TILE NIPPERS, FOR SHAPED CUTS

SANDPAPER OR TILE FILE

WORKBENCH OR OTHER SUITABLE CUTTING SURFACE (SEE PAGE 22)

MASKING TAPE, IF NEEDED

GETTING STARTED

Watch out for your eyes; remember to wear goggles to protect them from flying pieces of tile. You could also wear gloves to protect your hands.

A simple tile-scoring knife or tile cutter works well for straightforward tiling jobs. However, if you are working on a large area and are not only snapping tiles straight, but cutting them for corners or awkward spaces, then a jigsaw with tile-cutting blade is a good investment.

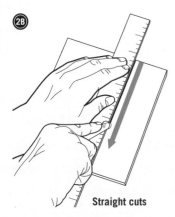

Straight cuts

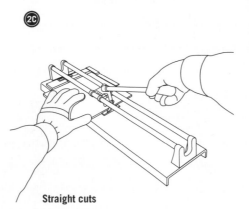

Straight cuts

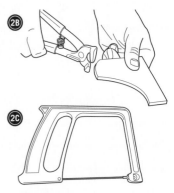

Shaped cuts

WHAT TO DO

Straight cuts

1 Measure and mark the line you want to cut along in china marker, all the way across the tile.

2 Cut the tile using one of the following options.

A Clamp tile to workbench and, wearing protective gloves, cut along line with jigsaw.

B Score tile with tile-scoring knife along marked line. Put on protective gloves and snap tile cleanly in two by hand, using firm and decisive motion.

C Use a tile cutter to score and snap the tile along the line.

3 Smooth all cut edges with sandpaper or a tile file.

Shaped cuts

1 Mark the line you want to cut along in china marker.

2 Cut the tile using one of the following options.

A Clamp tile to workbench and, wearing gloves, cut along line with jigsaw.

B Score with tile-scoring knife and use tile nippers to shape, nipping off pieces up to line.

C Clamp tile to workbench and cut with a tile saw.

3 Smooth cut edges with sandpaper or tile file.

HOW TO NAIL IT!

• It is very tricky to cut extra sections off a tile once you have made your cut, so cut once, cut right—measure, measure, and measure again. The key to shaping tiles is patience, but confidence, with every cut.

• You can place masking tape along the line to be cut before marking with pencil. This should stop the tile snapping in the wrong place.

• To snap a straight cut, hold the tile with scored line over edge of table and press firmly on either side. Alternatively, lay a pencil underneath the line and push down on either side.

TILE WALL

It's all about the preparation. Start tiling on a bumpy or "active" wall with pieces falling off it and don't be surprised if the result is a little disappointing. The wall should be clean, flat, and dry.

YOU'LL NEED

TILES, TO COVER AREA, PLUS EXTRA

STEEL TAPE MEASURE

PENCIL, PAPER, AND RULER

MASKING TAPE

WOODEN BATTEN OR OTHER SUITABLE LENGTH OF WOOD

STANDARD LEVEL

TILE ADHESIVE (PREMIXED OR POWDERED)

BUCKET OF WATER, IF USING PREMIXED ADHESIVE

NOTCHED TROWEL

TOOL UP SPACERS

TOOL DOWN MATCHES

MATERIALS FOR CUTTING TILES (SEE PAGE 36)

MATERIALS FOR GROUTING (SEE PAGE 34)

SILICONE CAULK AND CAULK GUN, IF NEEDED

GETTING STARTED

Measure, measure, and measure again. It's worth drawing areas on paper and checking again before starting. Always buy extra tiles; you will almost certainly get some cuts wrong.

Remember to leave spaces for grout and take your time.

To calculate number of tiles needed

Most tiles come in boxes or sheets enough to cover one square foot. Simply measure the length and width of area in feet and multiply to calculate the number of tiles to buy. Measure alcoves, bays, and L-shapes separately and add to the total. Add ten percent for wastage and mistakes.

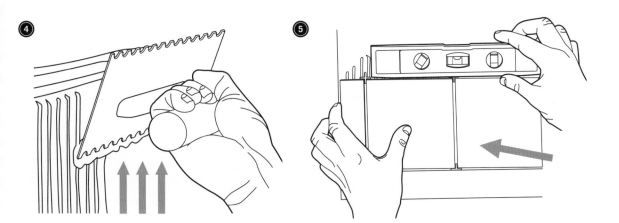

WHAT TO DO

1 Put plugs in the bath and sink and use masking tape to secure them.

2 Mark the area on the wall to be tiled, using pencil and wooden batten. Make sure lines are level using standard level.

3 If using powdered adhesive, mix it up according to the manufacturer's instructions.

4 Using the notched trowel, spread tile adhesive evenly over one square yard of wall at a time. Use the serrated edge to form ridges.

5 Start from the most visible corner and work across, one row at a time, sticking spacers or matches between each tile. Press each tile in place, twisting slightly as you press so that it beds in securely. Check that the tiles are level as you go. Work in sections. If you need a break, remove tile adhesive from areas not yet covered by scraping it off with the other side of the spreader and discarding.

6 Cut tiles as you go along (see page 36).

7 Leave adhesive to harden for 24 hours. Finish with grouting (see page 34) and caulk, if required (see page 46).

HOW TO NAIL IT!

- Always use cut tiles in corners where they will be less obvious.

- Never wash ANY tile adhesive or grout down the drain— it WILL harden and block the P-trap and you will have to cut out the section.

INSTALL MOSAIC TILES

Mosaic tiles have been around for many hundreds of years. Once placed one tiny tile at a time, they are now available in easy-to-fit sheets.

YOU'LL NEED

MOSAIC TILES TO COVER AREA, PLUS EXTRA

PENCIL

STANDARD LEVEL

TILE ADHESIVE (PREMIXED OR POWDERED)

BUCKET OF WATER, IF USING POWDERED ADHESIVE

NOTCHED TROWEL

TOOL UP CLEAN, DRY PAINT ROLLER

TOOL DOWN FLAT PIECE OF SCRAP BOARD AND SHORT LENGTH OF STRAIGHT WOOD

UTILITY KNIFE

STEEL TAPE MEASURE

DAMP SPONGE

MATERIALS FOR GROUTING (SEE PAGE 34)

GETTING STARTED

If you only plan to tile a section of wall, mark out the area using your pencil. Use a standard level to ensure that your lines are level.

If using powdered adhesive, mix it up according to the manufacturer's instructions.

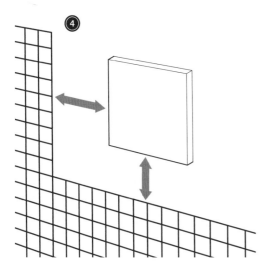

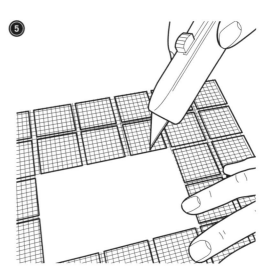

WHAT TO DO

1 Follow instructions for *Tile Wall* (see page 38), remembering to apply small areas of adhesive at a time and making sure that the wall to be tiled is clean and flat.

2 Apply the first sheet of mosaic tiles by pressing firmly into the adhesive and ensuring that the grout lines are level.

3 To make sure each tile beds into the adhesive, push the paint roller firmly over the area, or place scrap board over tiles and tap gently against the wall using a length of wood. Using a utility knife, cut the sheet of tiles to fit, if necessary.

4 To tile around an obstacle, such as a light switch, measure the distance from the last full sheet to the obstacle and measure the dimensions of the obstacle.

5 Use a utility knife to cut out tiles within the obstacle area.

6 Apply the cut sheet in the usual way.

7 Clean away excess adhesive from tile surfaces with a damp sponge. Leave tiles to set for at least 24 hours.

8 Finish with grouting (see page 34).

HOW TO NAIL IT!

- Check that each sheet of mosaic tiles is the right way up for your pattern before you apply it to the wall.

- Work quickly when applying the tiles to the adhesive; the backing sheet starts to disintegrate when in contact with adhesive, so it will become difficult to move.

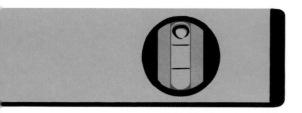

DRILL THROUGH TILES

06

Ceramic tiles are brittle but they can be drilled through without shattering. You need to use a ceramic tile or masonry drill bit to break through the glaze without skidding on, scratching, or cracking the surface.

▶ YOU'LL NEED

METAL/VOLTAGE DETECTOR
CHINA MARKER AND RULER
MASKING TAPE
⚠ POWER DRILL, WITH CERAMIC TILE AND WOOD OR MASONRY BIT
WALL ANCHOR(S)
SCREW(S)
TILE-SCORING KNIFE (OPTIONAL)

GETTING STARTED

These instructions are for drilling into tiles that are already fixed to the wall, so that an accessory, such as a towel hook, can be hung. Use a metal/voltage detector to check for water pipes and electricity cables before drilling.

WHAT TO DO

1. Mark desired point(s) on tile using china marker and ruler.

2. Place masking tape over marking(s), transferring it to top of tape if it doesn't show through.

3. Starting on a slow speed, drill hole with ceramic bit. Once through the tile, switch to the wood or masonry bit.

4. Remove masking tape and insert an appropriate wall anchor into hole. This should be a snug fit. Insert the fastener as required

5. If your accessory requires more than one screw, double-check the position of subsequent holes before repeating steps 2–4.

HOW TO NAIL IT!

- You can create a starter hole in the tile using a tile-scoring knife. This makes the drilling a little easier.

- Make a cross with two pieces of masking tape over the hole position for slightly more grip with drill bit.

REPLACE BROKEN TILES

If you only have one or two chipped or damaged tiles and a supply of spares to match, it's possible to remove and replace them.

YOU'LL NEED

SAFETY GLASSES OR GOGGLES
PROTECTIVE GLOVES
GROUT REMOVAL TOOL
⚠ POWER DRILL, WITH CERAMIC TILE OR MASONRY BIT
HAMMER
⚠ CHISEL
POWDERED TILE ADHESIVE
SMALL BUCKET OF WATER
NOTCHED TROWEL
◆ **TOOL UP** TILE SPACERS
◆ **TOOL DOWN** MATCHES
DAMP SPONGE
MATERIALS FOR GROUTING (SEE PAGE 34)

WHAT TO DO

Put goggles and gloves on, as broken tiles are sharp. Loosen grout around the edges of broken tile and rake it out. Also remove ³/₈ inch or so of grout in each direction around neighboring tiles.

❶ Drill holes in center of the broken tile to break it up a little more (see opposite).

❷ Remove pieces of tile using hammer and chisel, putting chisel into cracks and applying pressure with hammer. Work from center out to remove all tile pieces.

❸ Scrape away all tile adhesive remaining on wall surface.

❹ Mix a small amount of tile adhesive according to the manufacturer's instructions.

❺ Spread tile adhesive on back of replacement tile using notched side of trowel and fit into space on wall. Put tile spacers or matches in four corners to keep tile in position while adhesive dries.

❻ Wipe off any adhesive from tile surface with damp sponge.

❼ Finish with grouting. See *Grout Tiles* (page 34).

HOW TO NAIL IT!

- Be careful when chiseling the tiles. You don't want to dig into the wall—or yourself!
- Cracks in tiles allow moisture to get where it shouldn't, so replace broken or damaged tiles as soon as you can.

REMOVE SILICONE CAULK

Silicone caulk makes a great waterproof barrier but can be susceptible to mold and mildew. Dirty caulk can make your bathroom look ugly, and cleaning it is nearly impossible—so remove it and start again.

▶ YOU'LL NEED

UTILITY KNIFE

DAMP CLOTH AND GENTLE, NON-BLEACH CLEANER

AEROSOL LUBRICANT, SUCH AS WD-40; OR SILICONE CAULK REMOVER

▲ **TOOL UP** CAULK REMOVAL TOOL

▼ **TOOL DOWN** BLUNT UTILITY KNIFE OR SCRAPER

GLASS OR SAFETY SCRAPER

PLASTIC SCOURING PAD

 RUBBING ALCOHOL

GETTING STARTED

First check that what you're removing is actually silicone caulk. Use a utility knife to cut into it: If it's soft and rubbery, it is silicone and easily removable with your tools. If it's hard and crumbly, it is probably grout. See *Renovate Grout* (page 33).

Clean the whole area before you start, to remove soap scum and dirt. Use a damp cloth and gentle, non-bleach cleaner. If you clean after removing the silicone, water will find its way where it shouldn't.

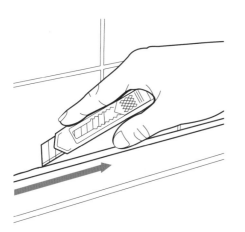

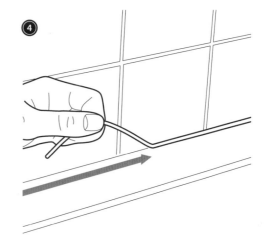

WHAT TO DO

1 Spray lubricant or caulk remover along the old caulk and leave for 5 minutes. The spray will start to break down the caulk, making it easier to take off. If you're using a specific caulk remover, refer to the instructions for timings.

2 Run your blunt knife or scraper, or caulk-removing tool, along the top and bottom edges of the seal. Be very careful not to scratch the tiles or bathtub.

3 Cut through the silicone at one end with the utility knife.

4 Lift up the end, grip it firmly and slowly, and pull the silicone away in one long thread. Use your knife to loosen any remaining pieces as you go. Be patient —you will save yourself time in the long run—but don't expect to do it all at once.

5 Scrape away remaining silicone with a glass scraper or safety scraper.

6 Use a plastic scouring pad soaked in rubbing alcohol to clean away any last traces of silicone.

HOW TO NAIL IT!

- Tread carefully with your tools to avoid damaging your tiles or bathtub.

- Be sure to remove all traces of old silicone before applying any more; new won't stick to old.

- Once you've cleaned away all remaining traces of old caulk, leave the surface completely clean and dry before applying new caulk.

APPLY SILICONE CAULK

09

Silicone caulk is ideal as a flexible and waterproof seal around sinks, bathtubs, and showers. It's easy to use and, if applied with care, can give an expert finish. Silicone comes in different colors, so if you have a colored suite or tiles, you should be able to find one to match.

YOU'LL NEED

MASKING TAPE

BATHROOM OR KITCHEN SILICONE CAULK AND CAULK GUN

UTILITY KNIFE

DISHWASHING LIQUID

TOOL UP CAULK SHAPER

TOOL DOWN YOUR FINGER

PAPER TOWELS

GETTING STARTED

To remove any old silicone caulk, see *Remove Silicone Caulk* (page 44).

Ensure that the surfaces are completely clean and dry before you start.

Choose a good-quality brand of caulk that has an anti-mold and anti-mildew ingredient.

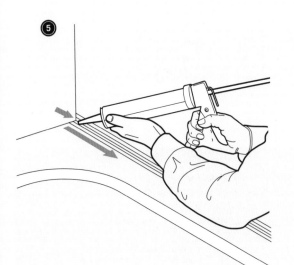

WHAT TO DO

1 Run some masking tape parallel to the edge of the area to be sealed, about ⅛ inch away. Do the same on the other side, ensuring that the gap between the two pieces of tape is even. This will help you keep a neat, straight line.

2 Place the tube of caulk into the caulk gun, then screw the nozzle onto the tube. Using your utility knife, cut the nozzle at a 45-degree angle to a size that corresponds with the area you are sealing. Cut a little off first; you can always cut more if needed.

3 Fill the bathtub with cold water. This prevents the caulk from being stretched and pulling away when you eventually have your well-earned bath.

4 Add a dash of dishwashing liquid to a small bowl of water and keep nearby.

5 Starting in the corner, squeeze the silicone steadily and smoothly along the space between the pieces of tape. Be generous and make sure that you don't leave any gaps. Don't worry about blobs; they will be neatened up next.

6 Dip the shaper or your finger into the bowl of water and dishwashing liquid. Starting from the same place you began, press the shaper or your finger into the silicone and drag it along between the tape, to make a concave line. Wipe off any excess on paper towels. Do about a foot at a time, then clean, re-wet, and repeat.

7 As soon as you're happy with the finish and have made sure there are no gaps, quickly remove the tape in one steady, even movement. Leave the silicone to set and the water in the tub for three to four hours. (Check specific timings against manufacturer's instructions.)

HOW TO NAIL IT!

- Where you cut the end of the applicator controls how much caulk comes out. For a small bead, cut the applicator near the tip; for a larger bead, cut higher up.

- Don't worry too much about mistakes, but if you are nervous, try applying a line on paper or cardboard before you begin, as a practice run.

- Start by applying short lengths of silicone until you gain confidence.

REMOVE AND PREVENT MOLD

Mold spores are everywhere in the air, but they will only grow in damp areas, caused mainly by household condensation. This is not only unsightly but it can be smelly, not to mention hazardous to your health.

YOU'LL NEED

RUBBER GLOVES
HOUSEHOLD BLEACH
PLUS, IF NEEDED:
RESPIRATOR
PLASTIC SHEETING AND TAPE
SOFT BRUSH
SPRAY BOTTLE
UTILITY KNIFE
PLASTIC WRAP
VACUUM CLEANER
MILDEW-RESISTANT PAINT AND PAINTBRUSH

GETTING STARTED

Wearing rubber gloves, test suspected mildew spots by dabbing a little household bleach onto the dark area. After one or two minutes, if it has lightened, it is probably mildew; if it remains dark, it is probably just dirt. Only do this on walls, not carpet. If you have a very large mold infestation (across more than one square yard, or with a strong, musty smell) take extra precautions to protect yourself and prevent spores from spreading. Wear old clothes and a respirator. Open doors and windows to outside and hang plastic sheeting over inner doorways.

WHAT TO DO

❶ Remove mold

Walls: wearing rubber gloves, mix one part bleach to eight parts water. Using a soft brush, scrub with bleach solution until mold disappears. Do not rinse surface. Leave to dry in direct sunlight, if possible.

Wallpaper: spray with water mist to stop spores spreading. Use utility knife to cut away moldy pieces in sections. Wrap in plastic and tape up for disposal. Vacuum away debris.

Carpets: it is difficult to clean mold from carpet and carpet pads. It's usually better to remove the carpet entirely.

❷ Prevent mold recurring

Find and fix any leaks or water access to area. Check and clear gutters, look at ventilation, and deal with causes of condensation. Allow area to dry fully, then repaint walls with mildew-resistant paint. See *Paint Walls* (page 150).

HOW TO NAIL IT!

- Never add another chemical substance to a bleached area. (Ammonia, even if hidden in a detergent, reacts with bleach to create a poisonous gas.)

- Poor insulation can aggravate condensation, which happens when hot, damp air meets a colder surface. You can help by limiting steam cooking, and drying clothes outside when possible. Keep doors and windows open when using bathroom, use extractor fans for 20 minutes after cooking, and increase ventilation.

- To tackle moldy grout, see *Renovate Grout* (page 33).

REMOVE LIME SCALE

11

Lime scale is the crystalline mineral deposit left behind when water evaporates. The best way to prevent lime scale from developing is to keep surfaces dry. Lime scale can be removed using natural acids like lemon juice, which are just as effective as man-made products.

YOU'LL NEED

WHITE VINEGAR OR LEMON JUICE
PLUS, IF NEEDED:
COTTON BALLS
RUBBER GLOVES
STRING
PLASTIC SCOURING PAD
LEMON, HALVED
TOOTHPICK
SCOURING SPONGE

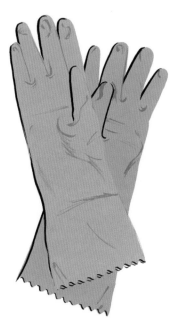

GETTING STARTED

Judge how serious your lime-scale deposits are and act accordingly!

WHAT TO DO

Washing machines and dishwashers

Run an empty wash cycle with a large cup of white vinegar or lemon juice instead of your usual detergent. Place liquid in base of dishwasher rather than in dispenser.

Electric kettles

1 Fill the kettle up to the lime-scale line (or quarter-full, if there is no strong line) with white vinegar or lemon juice. Leave to soak for an hour.

2 Fill kettle full with water and boil. Pour boiled solution away before it cools. Rinse kettle thoroughly several times.

Faucets

Soak cotton balls in vinegar or lemon juice. Wearing rubber gloves, wrap around lime-scaled parts–tie on with string if needed. Leave overnight, then wipe or scrub off.

Showerheads

1 Remove the faceplate from the showerhead—or just remove the whole showerhead. It should unscrew easily.

2 Soak faceplate or showerhead in white vinegar or lemon juice for at least eight hours. Alternatively, place the cut side of half a lemon against the shower head and tie it in place with string. Leave overnight and rinse.

3 Remove any remaining lime scale by pushing a toothpick through showerhead holes. Scrub clean. Replace showerhead.

Other flat surfaces

Scrub with scourer and vinegar or lemon juice, or rub with the cut side of half a lemon. Leave overnight and rinse.

HOW TO NAIL IT!

- For very thick lime-scale build-up you can chip it off carefully using a penknife tapped—very gently—with a hammer.

REPAIR CERAMIC OR ENAMEL SURFACE

Ceramic and enamel sinks, bathtubs, and toilets look great when they're shiny and new, but when they're chipped or cracked they not only look bad, but they can leak. Often, though, it's a simple job to repair them.

▶ YOU'LL NEED

SPONGE AND SCOURING PAD

DISHWASHING LIQUID

TOWEL

RUBBER GLOVES

TOOTHPICK OR RAZOR BLADE

⚠ PORCELAIN FILLER OR EPOXY PUTTY

KITCHEN SPATULA OR PUTTY KNIFE

COTTON BUD, IF NEEDED

NAIL-POLISH REMOVER, IF NEEDED

GETTING STARTED

Sponge-wash and scrub the sink, bathtub, or outside of toilet thoroughly with dishwashing liquid and hot water to get rid of grease and dirt. Dry it out completely with a towel.

WHAT TO DO

1 Wearing rubber gloves, use a toothpick or razor blade to spread the epoxy putty smoothly into the chipped or cracked area. Using a spatula or putty knife, scrape it flush to the surface and wipe away any excess.

2 Allow 24 hours for the putty to dry before touching the surface or exposing it to water.

HOW TO NAIL IT!

- Fix any rough epoxy edges using a cotton bud dipped in nail-polish remover. Do this while the epoxy is drying.

- Don't scrub the sink, bathtub, or toilet for a week after you've filled the cracks.

ADJUST LOOSE TOILET SEAT

Toilet seats can easily loosen through use, but you don't need to live with a seat that shifts to the side every time you sit down on it. Tightening it is easier than fitting a new seat—and it's a quick fix for an annoying problem.

YOU'LL NEED

SCREWDRIVER
ADJUSTABLE WRENCH OR PLIERS

GETTING STARTED

Find the bolts that secure the lid to the toilet at the back of the seat. They might be covered by plastic caps, which you can pop open.

WHAT TO DO

1. Use a screwdriver to tighten the bolts. If the bolt just spins in place, use a wrench or a pair of pliers to hold the nut on the underside firmly in place while turning the screwdriver.

2. Turn the nut clockwise to tighten and hold the bolt in place.

3. Check the toilet seat and adjust again, if necessary.

HOW TO NAIL IT!

- You can use a slotted screwdriver to help flip open the plastic caps.

- Don't overtighten the nuts or you risk cracking the seat —or worse, the toilet.

- It's often easier to take off the toilet seat, clean the toilet thoroughly, then refit.

REPLACE TOILET SEAT

This is the simplest toilet repair job around and it's a quick and easy way to make your toilet feel of new when you move to a new house.

YOU'LL NEED

STEEL TAPE MEASURE

NEW TOILET SEAT AND FASTENERS

**SCREWDRIVER
OR ADJUSTABLE WRENCH**

⚠ **BLEACH AND TOILET CLEANER**
PLUS, AS NEEDED:
**AEROSOL LUBRICANT,
SUCH AS WD-40**

MASKING TAPE

⚠ **JUNIOR HACKSAW**

GETTING STARTED

Check the shape and dimensions of your existing toilet seat before going to the hardware store. Toilet seats come in a few standard sizes. To be really sure, take your old seat with you.

WHAT TO DO

❶ Close the toilet lid and remove the seat from the toilet by unscrewing the fastening at the back. The bolts may be covered by caps, which you'll need to open first. Use fingers, a screwdriver, or wrench as needed.

❷ While the toilet is seat-free, clean it really well before putting on the new seat.

❸ Align the holes of the new seat with the holes of the toilet; insert the new bolts and fasten to secure.

❹ Secure the bolts with nuts on the underside and tighten with your screwdriver or wrench. Don't overtighten or you may crack the toilet. Add any caps.

HOW TO NAIL IT!

- If the nuts won't loosen, try spraying on lubricant, leaving a few minutes, and trying again.

- If the nuts are totally stuck, protect the toilet with masking tape and use a junior hacksaw to cut the bolts off. New toilet seats come with their own bolts so don't worry about destroying the old ones.

- **NEVER** mix chemical cleaners; dangerous reactions can occur.

UNCLOG TOILET

The only things you should flush down the toilet are things that would break down in a bucket of water if left for 24 hours. If your toilet does get clogged, it's worth trying to fix the problem yourself before calling a plumber.

YOU'LL NEED

RUBBER GLOVES
OLD NEWSPAPERS
PLASTIC JUG AND BUCKET
TOILET PLUNGER
WIRE COAT HANGER OR TOILET AUGER, IF NEEDED

GETTING STARTED

As soon as you notice a problem, use the toilet as little as possible. Don't flush repeatedly or it may overflow and flood the room!

WHAT TO DO

1. Put on rubber gloves.

2. Place old newspapers around the base of the toilet to catch any spills.

3. Bail out excess water from clogged toilet bowl into a bucket, using a plastic jug. You can pour this back down the toilet once it's clear.

4. Cover toilet with cup end of plunger, ensuring plunger is full of water. Push down firmly but carefully and lift slowly, repeating until blockage clears.

5. If blockage persists, try using a wire coat hanger. Unravel it and bend into a curve or snake shape. Push the wire up the toilet canal and wiggle it around to clear the blockage, being very careful not to scratch the toilet.

6. If the blockage persists, use toilet auger. Hold handle and insert wire into drain. Push gently while turning handle.

7. When crank becomes hard to turn, remove auger, clean end with running water and reinsert, repeating until blockage breaks up and clears.

8. When the blockage has cleared, flush toilet to check the flow.

HOW TO NAIL IT!

- Don't be too rough with your equipment; toilet bowls can easily be damaged.

- You may find that you need to clear the blockage from the other end—if so, find the manhole cover and use the toilet auger.

REPAIR TOILET FLUSH

16

If you've got problems with your toilet, there are a few easy things to try before calling the plumber. The most common issues tend to be that the toilet won't flush, or that water constantly runs into the cistern or bowl.

► YOU'LL NEED

OLD TOWEL

ADJUSTABLE WRENCH OR SLIP JOINT PLIERS

PLUS, AS NEEDED:

REPLACEMENT PARTS

SCREWDRIVER

SPONGE AND VINEGAR

GETTING STARTED

The first step is identifying the source of the problem. Have an old towel handy to mop up any spills. Take the tank lid off and flush the toilet a couple of times to watch the process. When you push the handle, the chain or rod lifts the flapper, or flap valve, allowing the water from the tank to fall through into the bowl. As the water in the tank drains, the float drops.

The float is connected to the inlet valve, which lets water into the tank when the float is down and should stop when the float is up. There is an overflow tube that drains water into the bowl if it gets too high.

There are a few standard kinds of replacement part, so it's best to remove the whole part, take it to your local hardware store, and buy one to match.

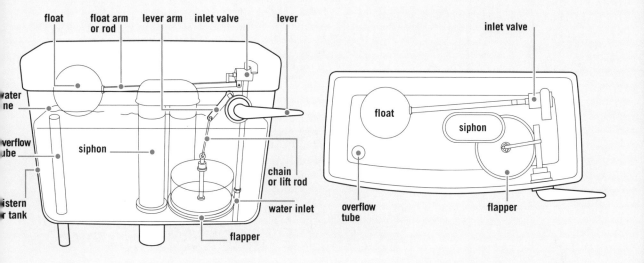

WHAT TO DO

If the toilet won't flush

Check that the flushing lever is still attached to the internal workings of the tank. It should be connected via a chain or lift rod. If isn't, reattach it or make a replacement from a thick piece of wire.

If the lever is loose

Tighten the nut on the inside of the tank that holds the lever to the tank.

If the lever or lever arm is broken

1 Remove the support nut attached to the lever. Unclip the chain or rod connecting the lever arm to the flapper and slide the lever and arm out of the hole in the tank.

2 Take the lever or lever arm to a hardware store and buy a replacement to match.

3 Feed the new arm and lever through the hole into the tank.

4 Tighten the support nut and reattach the chain or rod to the flapper.

If the tank keeps filling

If the tank keeps filling, the overflow will keep running, generally draining into the toilet bowl. This can waste a huge amount of water, so try to deal with it quickly.

1 Check the water level in the tank. It should be about 1 inch below the overflow outlet or in line with a marked water line inside the tank.

2 If it isn't, try adjusting the float down the arm or bending the float arm. Check to see if the water stops rising.

3 If this doesn't work, check whether the float is damaged and holding water. If it is, replace it.

4 If these steps don't solve the issue, there may be a problem with the inlet valve—the valve that lets water into the tank. Some have screws to manage the water level, so try adjusting these. You could also try cleaning the valve, but if it's worn or split, replace it.

If water is continuously flowing or leaking into the bowl

1 Check the water level of the tank—it may not be full enough. It should be about 1 inch below the overflow outlet or in line with a marked water line inside the tank. Increase the water level by turning the water valve all the way on. To find the water valve, look behind the tank of the toilet. It should be near the floor, usually on the left side of the toilet.

2 If this allows the tank to fill, the toilet should stop running and the problem will be solved.

3 If not, locate and check the flapper, or flap valve. This is the valve that sits at the bottom of the tank or underneath the siphon that lifts to let the water through to the toilet bowl. Over time, the rubbery part can get old and stiff, or lime scale can build up on it or around the valve (also called flush valve).

4 Run a finger carefully around the underside of the flapper and the rim where it sits. If you feel dirt, turn off the water valve and flush to empty the tank. Try cleaning with a sponge and some vinegar.

5 If the rubber is old and worn, replace it.

HOW TO NAIL IT!

- Ensure that the float isn't catching on anything or dragging against the side of the cistern.

- If these steps don't help solve the problem, you will need to call in a plumber to check for cracks or a worn gasket.

REPAIR LEAKY FAUCET

On older faucets, drips can often be stopped by replacing a washer. On many modern faucets, you may need to replace the interior cartridge that houses all the important parts.

YOU'LL NEED

- SCREWDRIVER
- PLIERS
- SLIP JOINT WRENCH, OR WRENCH TO FIT
- REPLACEMENT CARTRIDGE OR WASHER
- SILICONE GREASE
- HEAVY CLOTH, PIECE OF LEATHER, OR DUCT TAPE, IF NEEDED

GETTING STARTED

First, turn off the water supply. There is usually a valve under the sink or behind the shower assembly, or you may find a screw slot, which you'll need to turn with a screwdriver until it points across the width of pipe rather than along its length. Otherwise, turn off the water supply to the whole building.

Turn the faucet on and wait until you have cleared any residual water from the pipes.

Put the plug in the sink in case any small screws or nuts fall out while you're taking the faucet apart. It's a good idea to put these aside somewhere safe so that you can locate them easily when reassembling the faucet.

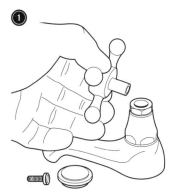
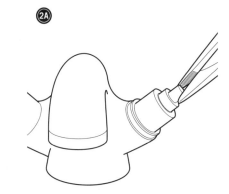
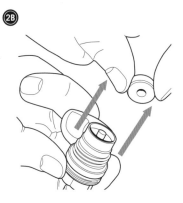

WHAT TO DO

1 Remove decorative handle cap (often marked "hot" or "cold"). Remove screw underneath, then jiggle the handle to remove. A screwdriver or slip joint pliers may be needed at any stage.

2 A *Modern faucets*: remove interior cartridge using pliers. Note: it may be held in by a lock ring or retaining nut that will need removing first, using a wrench. Replace with new cartridge.

B *Older faucets*: use wrench to undo retaining nuts, remove headgear, and reveal old washer. Prize out the washer and replace it with a new one.

3 Apply silicone grease to the screw threads, then reassemble the faucet in reverse sequence.

4 Turn water supply back on. Check for leaks in reassembled faucets.

5 If the problem continues, you may need to replace the faucet.

HOW TO NAIL IT!

- Use a cloth, piece of leather, or some duct tape to protect the faucet if using pliers on chrome surfaces.

- If the old washer is hard to remove, try levering it off with a screwdriver.

- Check that your replacement washer is exactly the same size and style as the old washer.

REPAIR DRIPPING SHOWERHEAD

A dripping showerhead doesn't just waste precious water, it can be extremely annoying. If your showerhead is cracked, rusty, or just falling apart, it's probably time to get a new one. However, if it appears to be in good condition, it's a simple job to repair it.

▶ YOU'LL NEED

- SCREWDRIVER
- WHITE VINEGAR OR LEMON JUICE
- TOOTHPICK
- SCOURING SPONGE
- MASKING TAPE
- REPLACEMENT WASHER OR CONNECTION
- PTFE OR PIPE WRAP TAPE, IF NEEDED

GETTING STARTED

First check that the showerhead is not split or damaged in any way and that the hose is securely screwed on.

Check the shower holes for lime-scale clogging, since this could be causing the dripping. Otherwise, a worn-out washer could be responsible.

The washer may have visible damage such as a split or break. It may also feel brittle and leave behind a dark residue on your fingers.

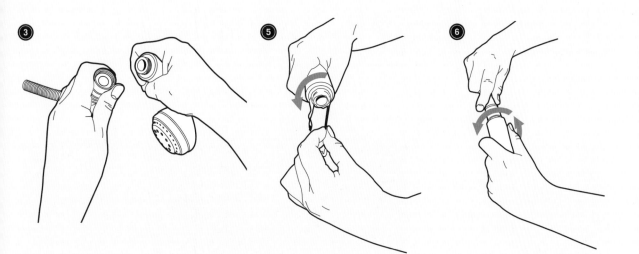

WHAT TO DO

1 Remove the faceplate from the showerhead. It should unscrew by hand.

2 To remove lime scale, soak faceplate in white vinegar or lemon juice for at least eight hours. Remove any remaining lime scale by pushing a toothpick through showerhead holes. Scrub clean with sponge scourer. See also *Remove Lime Scale* (page 49). Replace faceplate.

3 If this doesn't solve the dripping, you'll need to unscrew the showerhead from the hose. Before you do this, cover the drain with masking tape or put the plug into the bath.

4 Check the connection between hose and showerhead. Replace the rubber washer or connecting part as necessary.

5 Screw the hose back on and check. If shower still drips, try PTFE or pipe wrap tape; it helps make threaded fittings watertight. Unscrew head from hose and wrap tape around thread.

6 Screw hose and showerhead back together, tightening by hand.

7 Turn water on again and run shower briefly. Turn off, then wait a few minutes to check for drips. If the problem continues, you may need to buy a new showerhead or hose, or both.

HOW TO NAIL IT!

- Make sure your replacement washer is exactly the same size and style as the old washer.

UNCLOG SINK

Bathroom drains can easily get clogged with hair, kitchen sinks with waste food or vegetable peelings. You might need to remove the sink's P-trap to clear a blockage, or if you lose something valuable. Use chemical drain cleaner only as a last resort.

YOU'LL NEED

RUBBER GLOVES (OPTIONAL)
DAMP RAG OR CLOTH
PLUNGER
BUCKET
▲ **TOOL UP** SLIP JOINT PLIERS
▼ **TOOL DOWN**
ADJUSTABLE WRENCH

GETTING STARTED

Once you notice a clog, use the sink as little as possible so that you don't aggravate the problem. Gather all the tools you will need for the job before starting. Wear rubber gloves to help with grip and to protect your hands against any unpleasant waste.

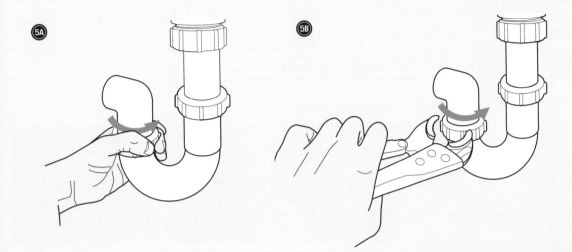

WHAT TO DO

1 Fill the clogged sink halfway with water, if not already full. Block overflow hole with damp rag or cloth.

2 Cover the sink drain opening with the cup end of plunger, ensuring that the plunger is full of water. Push down firmly but carefully and lift slowly, repeating until blockage clears.

3 When the blockage has cleared, run hot water down the sink drain for several minutes. Unblock the overflow hole.

4 If the blockage has not cleared, locate the P-trap—it's the U-shaped pipe that connects the vertical pipe coming from the sink to the horizontal pipe that goes into the wall. Place the bucket under the trap to catch any spills.

5 A Unscrew the trap.

B If too tightly fixed to unscrew by hand, use slip-joint pliers.

6 Pull away the trap; it will be full of dirty water so let it fall into the bucket.

7 Empty the trap into the bucket and look for any lost valuables. Clean the trap of any hair or food debris.

8 Reassemble the trap, taking care not to overtighten. Run hot water for several minutes to ensure that the clog has cleared. If the blockage persists, check outside drains.

HOW TO NAIL IT!

- If you lose something valuable down the sink, turn off the water as soon as possible so that the item doesn't get washed out of reach.

- Use sink strainers to help minimize future blockages.

- If the P-trap hasn't been loosened for a while and you need to use pliers or a wrench, protect the pipe with a cloth so you don't damage it.

CONNECT WASHING MACHINE OR DISHWASHER

20

These instructions assume that you are installing a new machine in place of an old one, and that all hot and cold water supplies, drains, and any drain-venting are already in place. If this is the case, this job should not take long, and with some plumbing know-how you can avoid calling in the professionals.

▶ YOU'LL NEED

NEW WASHING MACHINE OR DISHWASHER, PLUS HOSES

PLUS, AS NEEDED:

WASHING MACHINE OR DISHWASHER, INCLUDING ALL SUPPLY AND DRAIN HOSES

VALVE ADAPTERS OR GOOSENECK OR DISHWASHER 90 FITTING; HOSE CLIPS, IF NOT SUPPLIED

ADJUSTABLE WRENCH, CRESCENT WRENCH, OR PLIERS

GETTING STARTED

Remove all the packaging from outside and inside the appliance. Make sure you retain the instructions. Don't forget to recycle packaging wherever possible.

⚠ STAY SAFE!

Make sure your washing machine or dishwasher is not plugged in before you start work. Turn off the power at the circuit breaker to be safe.

For washing machines, remove bolts that secure drum while in transit, with adjustable wrench. For dishwashers, remove the cap from the drain-line connection.

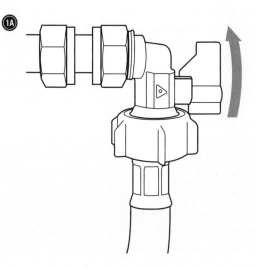

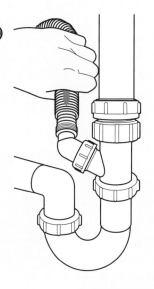

WHAT TO DO

1 Turn off the water and power supplies.

A *Washing machines*: For washing machines: connect the drain hose from the new machine into the existing drain. Attach drain hose to the appliance's drainage port and secure it with a hose clip. Put the other end of the drainage hose into the wall drain.

Find the hot and cold hoses on the back of the washing machine; these are usually held in place by hose clips. Screw each hose onto the appropriate faucet, then turn on each faucet and check that there are no leaks.

Plug in the washing machine and push it against the wall, leaving enough room for the hoses behind.

2 **B** *Dishwashers*: For dishwashers: attach the drain hose to the dishwasher. Use pliers to position any clips around the hoses and check that the connection is tight.

Attach any electrical wiring of the same color to the dishwasher's junction box—black to black, etc). Secure the wire nuts and close the junction box. Attach the copper ground wire beneath the round green ground screw.

Connect machine's water-supply hose to the water supply, following the manufacturer's instructions and using the supplied inlet hose. You may need to attach a gooseneck fitting or "dishwasher 90" connector to the dishwasher supply line.

Attach the drain hose to the plumbing system and tighten any clamps around the base of the hose.

Turn the water and power supplies back on.

HOW TO NAIL IT!

- Don't try to tackle any electrical jobs while connecting your machine. Call a professional electrician instead.

- If you are getting rid of an old washing machine or dishwasher, contact the manufacturer for advice on how to recycle it.

RENOVATE KITCHEN CABINETS

You can make a huge difference to the look of your kitchen with just some simple renovations to the cabinets. By repainting doors and updating the handles, you'll refresh the heart of your home without the need for a full redesign.

▶ YOU'LL NEED

- SCREWDRIVER
- STEEL TAPE MEASURE
- DROP CLOTH, NEWSPAPER, OR OLD CLOTHS
- RESPIRATOR OR DUST MASK
- SAFETY GOGGLES OR GLASSES
- FINE- AND MEDIUM-GRADE SANDPAPER
- ⚡ **TOOL UP** POWER SANDER
- ⚡ **TOOL DOWN** SANDING BLOCK
- SOFT CLOTH
- PAINTBRUSH
- PRIMER
- PAINT
- NEW DOOR HANDLES, HINGES, AND HARDWARE, AS DESIRED

GETTING STARTED

If you find it easier, use a screwdriver to remove your cabinet doors, drawer fronts, hinges and handles, and move them to your work space.

If you are replacing handles, take your old ones with you to the hardware store to ensure that you choose something with the same-size fittings. Remember to note down how many you'll need.

Also, if any of the handles were held on by more than one screw, note the distance between the two screws, since you will need to find replacement handles with the same distance between them. Otherwise, be prepared to fill and drill new holes.

It's a good idea to buy one sample first to check the fit before investing in a full set.

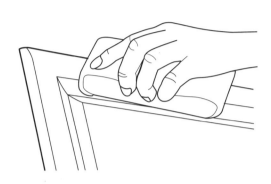

WHAT TO DO

1 Lay down a drop cloth, newspaper, or old cloths to protect your floor. Put on your respirator/dust mask and protective goggles or glasses.

2 Using medium-grade sandpaper, sand down the front and edges of wooden, painted, or varnished doors or drawer fronts with power sander (**A**) or sanding block (**B**). No sanding or priming is needed for melamine doors, but you do need to use the right paint. Wipe off dust and give the doors a good clean.

3 Paint on a coat of primer, leave it to dry, and apply another coat.

4 When dry, rub down surfaces with fine-grade sandpaper. Wipe off any dust.

5 Apply the first coat of paint and leave it to dry overnight. Repeat with another coat of paint for a more durable finish. See also *Paint Interior Woodwork* (page 168). Replace any old handles with new ones, if desired.

6 Replace doors and drawer fronts using a screwdriver to tighten the hinges.

HOW TO NAIL IT!

- If you have a number of cabinet doors to remove, label them on the back so that you can easily find the right place for the right door when you have finished.

- If your cabinet doors and drawer fronts do not completely cover the front of the cabinets, you can prepare and paint those surfaces in the same way. A good time to do this is while the cabinet doors are drying.

- To save time, buy a combined undercoat and primer and eliminate one of the stages.

REPAIR GRANITE COUNTERTOP

22

Granite is a great choice for a kitchen counter because it can withstand the heat of a saucepan and is easy to keep clean. It's a very durable material, but it is prone to chipping if you drop something hard on it. Fortunately, these chips can be fixed very easily.

► YOU'LL NEED

- SPONGE
- DISHWASHING LIQUID
- CLEAN, DRY DISH TOWEL
- MASKING TAPE
- RUBBER GLOVES
- ⚠ GRANITE EPOXY RESIN AND HARDENER
- KITCHEN SPATULA OR PUTTY KNIFE
- RAZOR BLADE
- GRANITE SEALER
- PAINTBRUSH

GETTING STARTED

Clean any grease and dirt from the damaged area with a sponge and warm, soapy water. Dry with dish towel and leave to air-dry for one hour.

Mask off the area to be repaired using masking tape.

WHAT TO DO

1. Wearing rubber gloves, mix up the epoxy resin and hardener, according to instructions.

2. Use a spatula or putty knife to apply resin to the damaged area.

3. Scrape off any excess with a razor blade.

4. Leave to dry for one hour, or as per instructions.

5. After 24 hours, apply granite sealer with a paintbrush. Leave to dry before using the countertop.

HOW TO NAIL IT!

- If the chipped area is in any way wet or greasy, it will not hold the resin.

- When you're scraping off the excess, hold the razor blade perpendicular to the countertop or you could risk pulling the resin out.

REPAIR LAMINATE COUNTERTOP

Laminate is one of the most affordable and popular materials for a kitchen counter. It comes in hundreds of different colors and styles. Small scratches, gouges, and chips can be disguised with the help of adhesive sealant.

YOU'LL NEED

- RUBBER GLOVES
- CLEAN RAG
- ⚠ SOLVENT
- KITCHEN SPATULA OR PUTTY KNIFE
- ADHESIVE SEALANT
- SPONGE
- DISHWASHING LIQUID

GETTING STARTED

Wearing rubber gloves, clean any grease and dirt from the damaged worktop area using a rag soaked in appropriate solvent. Check with your local hardware store to make sure it won't damage your counter surface.

Smooth down the surface as far as possible using a spatula to remove any fragments that are sticking out.

WHAT TO DO

1 Put a generous blob of adhesive sealant on the spatula or putty knife, gently press it down into the scratch, and smooth it out.

2 Repeat application until scratch has been filled and built up to level of countertop.

3 Smooth off the top with the spatula.

4 Use the solvent-moistened rag to wipe around sealed area.

5 Leave 24 hours for the sealant to harden before cleaning with sponge and warm, soapy water.

HOW TO NAIL IT!

- You may be lucky enough to find a sealant that matches the color of your laminate countertop. If not, opt for a clear one.

- If a strip of laminate has come loose from one of the front or side edges of the countertop, place a clean, folded dish towel over it and carefully press with a medium-hot iron. This should reactivate the glue so that it sticks back in place.

REPAIR WOODEN COUNTERTOP

24

The beauty of a solid wood countertop is that if you mistreat it and cause surface damage or scratches, you can simply sand it down and apply a few coats of oil to reveal a beautiful new surface.

YOU'LL NEED

MASKING TAPE

⚠ **TOOL UP** POWER SANDER

⬇ **TOOL DOWN** SANDING BLOCK

MEDIUM- AND FINE-GRADE SANDPAPER

DAMP CLOTH

RUBBER GLOVES

COTTON SWABS

⚠ HOUSEHOLD BLEACH

APPROPRIATE WOOD OIL, SUCH AS BUTCHER-BLOCK OIL

LINT-FREE CLOTH

GETTING STARTED

Allow any dark stains on wood to dry before starting work.

Look carefully over the worktop to locate all the marks you'll need to repair – knife marks are typical.

Use masking tape to protect taps and other areas that could get damaged by sandpaper.

WHAT TO DO

1 Using power sander or sanding block, sand carefully over the areas to be repaired. Start with medium-grade sandpaper, then smooth off with fine-grade sandpaper.

2 Remove dust from sanded surfaces with a damp cloth. Leave to dry.

3 Wearing rubber gloves, use cotton swabs dipped in bleach to remove any remaining black stains. Apply and leave for one hour to work.

4 Apply wood oil using a lint-free cloth. Leave overnight or at least eight hours to dry.

5 Sand down gently using fine-grade sandpaper.

6 Repeat steps 4 and 5 until two coats have been applied. Apply third coat and leave to dry.

HOW TO NAIL IT!

• For a thorough job, remove the silicone from the joint between the countertop and wall before sanding, then reapply when you have finished (see pages 44 and 46).

DOORS

AND

WINDOWS

EVERYTHING YOU NEED TO GET THE JOB DONE

RESIZE INTERIOR DOOR

Over time, moisture in the air can cause doors to swell and become hard to open. Sometimes, they stick because they've been painted too often. Sanding or planing off some of the door can bring it back to its full use. Use a helper for best results.

YOU'LL NEED

DOOR WEDGES

SCREWDRIVERS

PLIERS

COARSE- AND MEDIUM-GRADE SANDPAPER

⚡ **TOOL UP** POWER SANDER

⚡ **TOOL DOWN** SANDING BLOCK

⚡ **TOOL UP** POWER PLANER

⚡ **TOOL DOWN** PLANER

WORKBENCH, OR OTHER SUITABLE SURFACE (SEE PAGE 22)

PAINTBRUSH

WOOD PRIMER

PAINT

GETTING STARTED

Examine all the door edges to find the area that's sticking. Check for scrape marks on paint or wood.

If the sticking point is on the top or upper edge, you should be able to fix the door in position. If it is sticking near the floor, remove the door from its hinges and clamp it to a workbench.

To remove the door, open it and put wedges or screwdrivers underneath to hold it off floor. With a helper, unscrew the hinges from the frame and carefully lift the door away.

If your door has hinge pins, wedge the door, then use pliers to remove the bottom hinge pin, then the top one. Lift door up and away. Sometimes a door will separate itself from the frame as soon as pins are removed, so be careful.

WHAT TO DO

1 Tackle the sticking point

A *For small areas:* sand away a high spot with coarse-grade sandpaper and block.
B *For larger, high areas:* use planer to shave off excess wood. Sand with medium-grade sandpaper or a power sander.

2 Prime the wood and repaint it. See *Paint Interior Woodwork* (page 168).

3 To rehang the door, screw hinges back on the door. With a helper, lift the door into position and screw in the frame hinges. For hinge pins, position door in frame and hold it in place with wedges or screwdrivers. Have your helper hold the door while you replace the top hinge pin first, then the lower one.

HOW TO NAIL IT!

- If you need to use the planer close to the lock, remove the lock first to avoid damaging it. Simply unscrew and pull away.

- Never remove more than $3/8$ inch from each side of a door, and not more than $1/4$ inch from a panel door, or you will weaken its structure.

1B

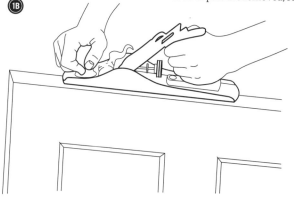

REPLACE DOOR HINGES

Door hinges can get squeaky or unstable with age. See *Fix Squeaky Door* (page 72), as a first step to resolving squeaks. Replacing them is a relatively straightforward way to relieve stress on your door. Use a helper for best results.

YOU'LL NEED

DOOR WEDGES

SCREWDRIVERS

PLIERS, IF NEEDED

NEW HINGES

⚠ **POWER DRILL, WITH WOOD DRILL BIT, IF NEEDED**

⚠ **CHISEL AND MALLET, IF NEEDED**

GETTING STARTED

Remove the old hinges (see step 1) and take them to the hardware store before buying replacements. This way, you'll know you're buying exactly the right size and quantity.

WHAT TO DO

❶ Put door wedges or screwdrivers under door to hold it open. For fixed hinges, unscrew the hinges from the doorjamb. With a helper, pull the door away and unscrew hinges from it. Remove hinge pins following instructions, opposite.

❷ Buy replacements.

❸ To rehang, screw new hinges on door first, then lift into position with helper and screw into original holes on doorjamb. For hinge pins, hold door in position and put pin in.

❹ If your new hinges are a different size, or if you need to reposition the hinge, you may need to drill new small pilot holes first in the door and jamb before screwing into place. Use a chisel to create recesses on door and jamb as necessary, to fit.

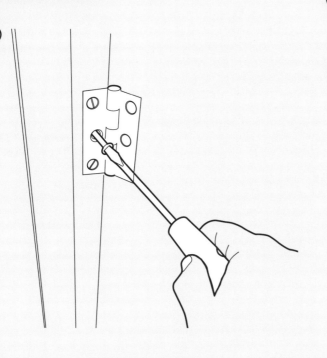

HOW TO NAIL IT!

• The number of hinges needed will depend on the weight of the door, so don't skimp by replacing three hinges with two.

FIX SQUEAKY DOOR

27

Squeaky doors always seem to be at their worst at night, when you're trying to be quiet, but at any time of day, the noise is very annoying. Whether the squeak comes from the hinge or the handle, it's usually a very easy job to fix.

▶ YOU'LL NEED

WARM, SOAPY WATER
SOFT CLOTH
TOOL UP AEROSOL LUBRICANT, SUCH AS WD-40
TOOL DOWN OLIVE OIL AND PAINTBRUSH OR CLOTH
PLUS, AS NEEDED:
PLIERS
STEEL WOOL AND SOAP
HAMMER

GETTING STARTED

Figure out which part of the door the squeak is coming from.

Make sure the hinges are free of dust and grime by wiping with warm, soapy water.

WHAT TO DO

1 Spray lubricant or dab a small amount of olive oil onto the hinge mechanism.

2 Open and close door a few times to allow lubricant or oil to work its way through.

3 Wipe away excess.

4 If your door has hinge pins and is still squeaking, remove one pin at a time with pliers. See *Resize Interior Door* (page 70). Wipe with steel wool and rub with soap. If bent, tap into shape with hammer. Replace and repeat with second pin. Alternatively, replace with new.

HOW TO NAIL IT!

- Using olive oil rather than an aerosol lubricant is not only better for the environment, but smells much nicer. Avoid using vegetable oils; they oxidize, turning rancid and sticky.

INSTALL PET DOOR

Electronic pet doors that work with magnets are a popular option but they can allow other cats or dogs with magnetic collars to get into your house. They can also attract metallic debris. Smart pet doors allow access to your pets only, as long as they bear the matching smart key on their collars.

YOU'LL NEED

- STEEL TAPE MEASURE
- PET DOOR TO FIT YOUR PET, WITH TEMPLATE AND FASTENERS
- MASKING TAPE
- STANDARD LEVEL
- ⚠ POWER DRILL & WOOD BITS
- PENCIL AND LONG RULER
- ⚡ **TOOL UP** POWER JIGSAW
- ⚡ **TOOL DOWN** KEYHOLE SAW
- MEDIUM-GRADE SANDPAPER
- SCREWDRIVER
- ⚠ JUNIOR HACKSAW, IF NEEDED

GETTING STARTED

Refer to the manufacturer's instructions before you start.

WHAT TO DO

❶ Choose a position the pet will be able to reach, in a thinner part of the door, if possible. This should be about 3–6 inches off the ground for a cat or small dog, as a rough guide. Tape the template in position on the door and, using a standard level, check that it's level.

❷ Drill holes at each inner corner of the catflap template, using a ½ inch bit. This is to mark where you will cut out the inner slot.

❸ Remove template and draw lines connecting holes using a pencil and ruler.

❹ Insert the jigsaw or the keyhole saw into a corner hole and cut along the lines to remove the panel and reveal the hole. See *Install Mail Slot* (page 74). Smooth out rough edges with medium-grade sandpaper.

❺ Hold flap in position over hole and make sure it's level. Mark and drill screw-fixing holes through door with ⅜ inch bit, or one recommended by the manufacturer.

❻ Screw the pet door sections in place and fasten it with the screws and nuts supplied.

HOW TO NAIL IT!

- If the supplied bolts are too long for your door, fit the nuts, then cut bolts to size with a hacksaw.

- Make sure you install the pet door the right way around; otherwise your pet may be able to get in, but not out.

- You can also install a pet tunnel in a solid wall. If you want to install in glass, contact a local glass or window dealer to make the hole.

INSTALL MAIL SLOT

29

This is a straightforward job, but remember to double-check all your measurements before drilling a hole in your front door.

YOU'LL NEED

- **MAIL SLOT AND MOUNTING HARDWARE**
- **PENCIL**
- **LONG RULER**
- **STANDARD LEVEL**
- ⚠ **POWER DRILL, WITH APPROPRIATE DRILL BITS**
- ⚡ **TOOL UP** POWER JIGSAW
- ⚡ **TOOL DOWN** KEYHOLE SAW
- **MEDIUM-GRADE SANDPAPER**
- **SCREWDRIVER**
- ⚠ **JUNIOR HACKSAW, IF NEEDED**

GETTING STARTED

First decide on the position of the mail slot. US Postal Service guidelines state that it must be a minimum of 30 inches from the ground, so that postal workers can reach it without difficulty.

If your door is paneled, you must fit your mail slot to a strong, non-paneled section of the door. If you have a solid wood door, the mail slot can go anywhere, as long as it's the correct distance from the ground. Most people install mails slots in the center of the door, just below the door handle.

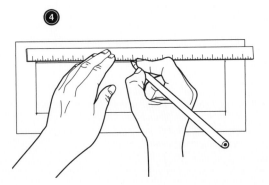

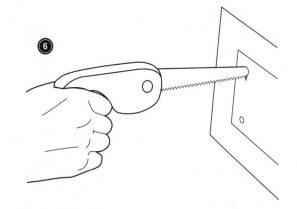

WHAT TO DO

1 Find the center of the door at the height you have chosen and mark with pencil.

2 Center the mail slot along the mark and draw around the outside of it with your pencil.

3 Measure the distance between the outside edge of the mail slot and the top, bottom, and sides of the inner flap. Make a note of these, then mark the inner measurements on the door.

4 Connect your pencil marks using a pencil and ruler so that the inner flap and its position are now clearly outlined on the door. Double-check that the outline is straight using a standard level.

5 Drill starter holes at each inside corner of the inner flap, using a ½ inch bit.

6 Insert saw into a corner hole and carefully cut along the pencil lines to remove the inner panel.

7 Smooth out rough edges with medium-grade sandpaper.

8 Carefully measure from the edges to the center of the bolt fasteners (lug holes) on the mail slot, then mark these positions on the outline on the door. Match the bolt size supplied to a twist drill bit, then start drilling on one side of the door. When the drill protrudes, finish off from the other side.

9 Insert the mail slot into the door and fasten it in place with the bolts supplied.

10 Screw mail slot cover to the inside of the door, if supplied.

HOW TO NAIL IT!

- If the supplied bolts are too long for your door, fit the nuts, then cut bolts to size with a hacksaw. Be careful to leave enough length to attach the nuts securely.

- If the supplied bolts are too short, use a larger drill bit and countersink the nuts. See *Back to Basics* (page 18).

INSTALL DOOR CASING

Door casing or trim, also known as architrave, is the timber molding that hides the joint between the door frame and the wall. Adding one to your door frame is a simple matter of cutting and fixing three lengths of molding.

▶ YOU'LL NEED

PENCIL AND RULER

DOOR CASING MOLDING, TO FIT THREE SIDES OF DOOR FRAME

TOOL UP COMPOUND MITER SAW

TOOL DOWN MITER BOX AND BACKSAW

⚠ GRAB ADHESIVE

FINISH NAILS

HAMMER

WOOD GLUE

NAIL PUNCH

DAMP CLOTH

CAULK AND CAULK GUN

FINE-GRADE SANDPAPER

PAINTBRUSH

PRIMER

PAINT

GETTING STARTED

If you're also installing baseboards to your room, install the door casing first.

Using a pencil and ruler, mark points ¼ inch away from door frame at intervals all around frame (**A**). Draw a continuous line through these points. This is where your casing molding will be positioned.

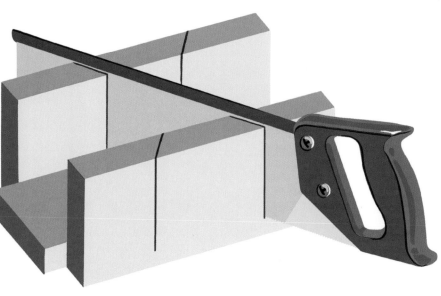

WHAT TO DO

1 Hold length of casing beside the edge of the door jamb. Mark the level of the top corner of the door in pencil on the casing.

2 Cut 45-degree angle at the marked point using a miter saw, or miter block and saw. See *Install Baseboards* (page 132). Before you cut, make sure the angle is facing the right way. For the upright casings, it should go upwards and outwards, with the lowest part starting from the side of the casing closest to the door.

3 Repeat with other lengths of casing, remembering to cut two miters from each end of the overhead length and checking the angle before you cut.

4 Apply a line of grab adhesive to the back of one vertical length of molding. Place the casing with the molded edge facing the doorway on your ¼ inch line.

5 Loosely fix the casing with one or two finish nails, but don't hammer them in all the way.

6 Repeat steps 4 and 5 with the second vertical casing.

7 Apply line of grab adhesive to back of overhead casing and apply wood glue where the miters meet. Place overhead casing in position, adjusting the side sections to get a good fit.

8 Nail all three sections in place, banging the finish nails in all the way, every 12–16 inches, with a nail punch.

9 Wipe away any adhesive. Use caulk to fill any discrepancies in the miters, behind the casing or over the nail holes (see *How to Nail It!*, page 133). Sand down when dry.

10 Prime and paint to finish. See *Paint Interior Woodwork* (page 168).

HOW TO NAIL IT!

- Don't hammer the finish nails in all the way or you risk damaging the casing with the hammer. Finish off the job with a nail punch.

- If you want to save time on painting, buy ready-primed MDF door casing molding.

- If your doorway is not quite "true"—i.e. not straight vertically and horizontally—it's often best to follow the line of your door.

INSTALL DOORBELL

Some doorbells are battery-powered and wireless and really easy to install. Others take a small amount of wiring, but if you're replacing an old one, this can be done without an electrician. If in any doubt, however, consult a professional.

▶ YOU'LL NEED

DOORBELL KIT, WITH FIXINGS
BATTERIES, IF NEEDED
⚠ **POWER DRILL, WITH MASONRY AND WOOD BITS, AS NECESSARY**
SCREWDRIVER
MULTIPURPOSE DETECTOR
WALL ANCHORS, IF NEEDED
HAMMER
PINS AND PLASTIC CLIPS

GETTING STARTED

Doorbells are generally supplied as two components: the button and the bell or chime. Both require power, which can come from batteries or your household wiring. They can be connected to receive the same power source, or powered separately by a combination of batteries and domestic electricity.

Determine whether your bell will be powered by batteries or wiring and whether the button and bell will be wired together or communicate wirelessly. If you don't already have electric wiring for a doorbell, a battery-powered or plug-in device is best.

Battery-powered: these are easy to install because as you don't need to worry about tapping into your electricity supply. You will need to replace the batteries periodically, however.

Electrically powered: If you are replacing an existing bell, you just need to do some simple wiring. If you are installing an electric doorbell for the first time, you will need an electrician to run a wire out of the main household circuit for you.

Combination: some modern doorbell units communicate wirelessly, so each component needs its own power source. The button is powered by batteries, and the bell is either battery-powered or plugged in to a normal household socket. This combination style is the easiest to install, since you don't need to connect any wires.

Choose the best place for the bell unit to be installed. This should be somewhere that will be heard through the house, like a hallway.

⚠ STAY SAFE!
Before attempting to connect wiring to your power supply, turn off your electricity supply. If in any doubt, consult a professional.

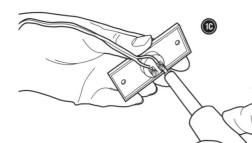

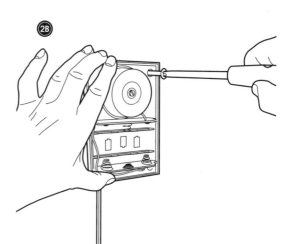

WHAT TO DO

① Install the button

A If you're installing a wired device, choose a position on the door frame at chest height and drill a small hole all the way through frame for the wire. Drill small pilot holes for screws.

B For wired mechanism, pass wires through hole from inside to outside.

C Strip back any insulation and connect the wires to the button unit, following manufacturer's instructions.

D Screw the backplate of button unit onto door frame and secure the front cover.

E Install batteries (if needed) to the button unit, according to the manufacturer's instructions.

② Install the bell unit

A Check chosen position for pipes and cables using a multipurpose detector and locate studs, if you're not fitting the bell to masonry. Hold the bell unit in place and mark positions for the screws.

B Drill holes to depth of wall anchors, if using, and insert. Screw the backplate to the wall.

C If your unit is powered, turn off your electricity first. For wired mechanisms, strip back the insulation on the ends of the wire and join the wire from the button to the bell unit.

D Replace the bell unit cover. Connect the existing wiring following the manufacturer's instructions.

E Secure the wire discreetly alongside door frame or baseboard as appropriate, using a hammer, finish nails, and small plastic clips.

HOW TO NAIL IT!

- If the wiring has any kinks in it, try warming it by rubbing your hands over it a few times. This should allow it to be smoothed out.

- Change batteries as soon as they have run down; if they stay in place, they may corrode and damage the main unit.

- Try to keep the wire between battery-powered units as short as possible. The farther the electricity has to travel, the faster your batteries will run out.

INSTALL DOOR KNOCKER

Fitting a front door knocker is a straightforward job and is also a quick way to give the front of your house a makeover. There are many different styles out there, so choose one that blends well with the other parts and design of your door.

▶ YOU'LL NEED

DOOR KNOCKER, WITH HARDWARE

STEEL TAPE MEASURE

PENCIL

SCRATCH AWL OR NAIL

⚠ **POWER DRILL, WITH WOOD BITS TO MATCH BOLT SIZE**

SCREWDRIVER

⚠ **JUNIOR HACKSAW**

GETTING STARTED

Choose the position for your knocker. It will probably look best centered, so measure the width of the door to find the midpoint. Choose a good height. Mark chosen point with pencil.

WHAT TO DO

1. Measure the door knocker and note the distance between any fasteners.

2. Use measurements to mark hardware positions on the door with a scratch awl or nail, on each side of the central point. Repeat the measurements to double-check for accuracy.

3. Starting from one side, drill most of the way through the hardware marks, then finish the holes from the other side. This will help keep the wood from splitting as the drill comes through. Blow any sawdust out of holes.

4. Screw the knocker into door and tighten the nuts and bolts. Trim any excess bolt length with a hacksaw.

HOW TO NAIL IT!

- Make sure you drill through the door in a straight line, not at an angle.

- Before you fully tighten any screws, check that the knocker is hanging straight.

- Keep your fingers out of the way when using a hacksaw.

INSTALL DRIP CAP

A drip cap is a slanted piece of wood or metal at the bottom of your external door. It keeps water away from your door frame and prevents it from running back into your house. It's worth installing one if your door is regularly exposed to harsh weather, because it's easier to replace a drip cap than a whole door!

YOU'LL NEED

STEEL TAPE MEASURE

DRIP CAP MOLDING, TO FIT MEASUREMENTS

⚠ **HANDSAW OR BACKSAW, IF NEEDED**

WORKBENCH OR OTHER SUITABLE CUTTING SURFACE (SEE PAGE 22)

FINE-GRADE SANDPAPER

PAINTBRUSH

WOOD PRIMER, IF NECESSARY

PAINT, IF NECESSARY

PENCIL

⚠ **POWER DRILL, WITH WOOD BIT AND COUNTERSINK OR LARGE BIT**

SCRATCH AWL OR NAIL

WOOD GLUE OR GRAB ADHESIVE

WOOD SCREWS

SCREWDRIVER

GETTING STARTED

Measure the width of the door from the outside, with door in closed position. Subtract ⅜ inch from measurement to ensure the drip cap won't catch on the frame as the front door closes. Make a note of the measurement.

WHAT TO DO

❶ Ideally, buy drip cap molding to fit, or cut to size with handsaw or backsaw. Sand down for a smooth finish.

❷ Prime and paint the back and bottom of the drip cap, if necessary. Wait until dry.

❸ Hold the drip cap in position against the door, making sure the bottom of the drip cap is level with the bottom of the door, but not touching the sill. Mark the top of drip cap onto the door in pencil.

❹ On a workbench or suitable surface, drill three or four evenly spaced pilot holes through narrowest part of drip cap (at the front, near top).

❺ Countersink the pilot holes, if necessary. See *Back to Basics* (page 18).

❻ Hold drip cap in place and mark through holes with scratch awl or nail. Remove and drill pilot holes at marks to depth of screw —don't go through door.

❼ Apply glue or adhesive to the drip cap back. Line it up against the pencil mark and screw to door, sinking screws all the way into wood. If the cap catches, sand it down until the door opens smoothly.

❽ Prime and paint the cap to match door. See *Paint Exterior Woodwork* (page 170).

HOW TO NAIL IT!

• A hardwood drip cap will last longer than one made from soft wood, but check what the door is made from first; there's little point in fitting a hardwood drip cap to a softwood door, since the drip cap will outlast the door!

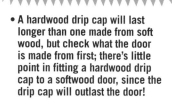

REPAIR ROTTEN WINDOW FRAME

34

Weather will eventually take its toll on wooden window frames. If paint wears away and moisture is allowed to get in, the wood underneath can get damp and will crack and rot. Repair damaged areas as soon as possible to stop the spread.

▶ YOU'LL NEED

PENKNIFE

⚠ **CHISEL OR NARROW SCRAPER**

⚠ **WOOD PRESERVATIVE**

PAINTBRUSH

RUBBER GLOVES

EXTERIOR WOOD REPAIR COMPOUND

PUTTY KNIFE

WATERPROOF OUTDOOR WINDOW CAULK OR SEALANT, IF NEEDED

COARSE- AND MEDIUM-GRADE SANDPAPER

⚡ **TOOL UP** POWER SANDER

⚡ **TOOL DOWN** SANDING BLOCK

WOOD PRIMER AND EXTERIOR-GRADE PAINT

GETTING STARTED

Test for rot by poking a penknife into the wood. It will sink easily into rotten wood. Identify the areas for replacing this way.

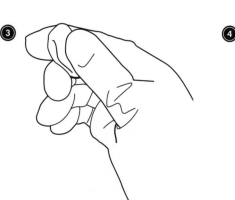

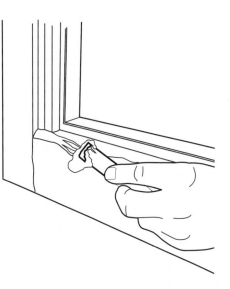

WHAT TO DO

1 Remove all rotten wood using chisel or scraper. Dig down until the wood is sound, but don't damage healthy wood. Clean away all the debris.

2 Ensure that the area is fully dried out. Paint wood preservative over the whole window frame surface.

3 Wearing rubber gloves, knead the repair compound.

4 Use a putty knife to apply the repair compound in layers to the damaged area. Press in well to avoid air bubbles. Keep going until the putty is worked up to the level of the rest of frame.

5 Seal any gaps between the frame and wall with waterproof window sealant.

6 Leave sealant to dry for 48 hours.

7 Using power sander or sandpaper and block, sand entire window frame with coarse-grade, then medium-grade sandpaper so that the only difference between the repaired area and the original frame should be color.

8 Prime and paint window frame in chosen color. For the best finish, use two coats in your chosen color. See *Paint Exterior Woodwork* (page 170).

HOW TO NAIL IT!

- Work on a dry day when the weather won't be competing against your hard work.

- If more than ten percent of your window frame is rotten, the structure isn't sound and the whole frame will need to be replaced.

REPLACE BROKEN WINDOWPANE

Broken glass doesn't just let the weather in or heat out; it can also be dangerous and a security risk. You should be able to replace small panes of glass yourself, but you'll need to get a whole new unit made if your window is insulated (such as Thermopane)—i.e. two panes of glass separated by an air space.

▶ YOU'LL NEED

- NEWSPAPER OR OLD SHEET
- PROTECTIVE WORK GLOVES
- SAFETY GLASSES OR GOGGLES
- HAMMER, IF NEEDED
- STEEL TAPE MEASURE
- HARDWOOD OR PLYWOOD, IF NEEDED
- ⚠ JUNIOR HACKSAW, IF NEEDED
- WORKBENCH OR OTHER SUITABLE CUTTING SURFACE (SEE PAGE 22)
- FINISH NAILS OR EXTERIOR SILICONE CAULK OR SEALANT, IF NEEDED
- REPLACEMENT PANE OF GLASS
- ⚠ CHISEL, IF NEEDED
- PUTTY KNIFE
- PLIERS, IF NEEDED
- MEDIUM-GRADE SANDPAPER AND SANDING BLOCK
- WOOD SEALANT
- PAINTBRUSH
- WOOD PRIMER
- GLAZING COMPOUND (PUTTY)
- FINISH NAILS OR GLAZIER'S PUSH POINTS
- LINSEED OIL
- EXTERIOR-GRADE PAINT

GETTING STARTED

Wear sturdy boots to protect your feet from broken glass.

If the windowpane is smashed, lay down newspaper or old sheet on both sides of window. Put on protective gloves and goggles. Work each piece of glass loose, from top down. Tap any remaining glass out with hammer. Wrap in newspaper to dispose of.

Measure space for replacement pane in a few locations in case the wood is warped or uneven. Measure to the recess that holds the pane and subtract ⅛ inch from height and width to ensure the pane will fit easily.

For a temporary repair, cut a piece of hardwood or plywood to fit. Secure with finish nails or weatherproof silicone caulk/sealant.

If the pane is only cracked, seal cracks with silicone sealant.

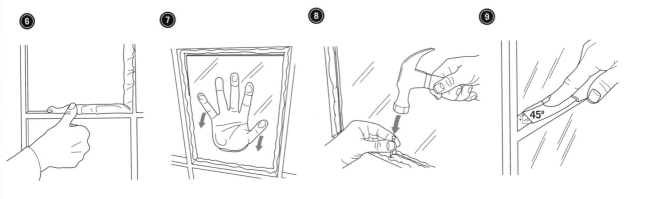

WHAT TO DO

1 Lay the new pane on a pad of newspaper (not a hard surface) well away from your working area.

2 If the cracked pane is still in place, remove the glazing compound so that you can take out whole pane. Chip out old putty using a chisel or putty knife, taking out nails or push points with pliers as you go along. Save any that can be reused.

3 Sand down the exposed wood, fill in any holes or cracks with wood sealant, and paint with wood primer.

4 Clean out any debris from the recess and wet your hands to prevent the glazing compound from sticking.

5 Knead the compound until it is pliable and take a palm-sized ball to work with.

6 Roll compound into long strip. Place this along the recess and press down with your thumb to a thickness of around 1/8 inch.

7 Set the new pane into the bottom edge of frame and gently push it into place in the putty. Allow putty to squish out of the recess to form a weatherproof seal.

8 Secure glass by carefully tapping finish nails or glazier's push points into the compound, flat against surface of glass. Space nails at 1-inch intervals.

9 Roll another worm of compound and press firmly into edges. Wet putty knife and smooth compound neatly with the knife at a 45-degree angle, so nails or push points are covered. If knife sticks, dip into linseed oil, wipe off excess, and use again.

10 Remove surplus compound from both sides of the glass with the putty knife.

11 Leave compound for two weeks to harden, then prime and paint window frame. See *Paint Exterior Woodwork* (page 170).

HOW TO NAIL IT!

- Save a piece of the broken pane to take to the glass dealer or glazier to ensure that you order the right thickness. If in doubt, it's always better to buy thicker glass rather than thinner.

- If the old compound is hard to remove, use a heat gun, soldering tool, or hairdryer to soften it.

- If you need to remove excess oil from the new glazing compound, roll it over some newspaper before using.

CURTAINS AND BLINDS

EVERYTHING YOU NEED TO GET THE JOB DONE

INSTALL CURTAIN ROD

Curtain rods can be decorative features in themselves, so choose carefully and think about how they'll blend in with other features in the room.

▶ YOU'LL NEED

STEEL TAPE MEASURE

CURTAIN, WITH RINGS OR LOOPS

CURTAIN ROD AND HARDWARE

⚠ **JUNIOR HACKSAW, IF NEEDED**

WORKBENCH OR OTHER SUITABLE CUTTING SURFACE (SEE PAGE 22)

MULTIPURPOSE DETECTOR

PENCIL

LONG STANDARD LEVEL

⚠ **POWER DRILL, WITH SUITABLE BITS**

SCREWS AND WALL ANCHORS, AS NEEDED

SCREWDRIVER

GETTING STARTED

Choose position and length of curtain rod. Make sure curtains can be pulled back at least 2 inches from the edge of the window to allow for maximum light. Heavy fabric will take up more space.

Choose the height of curtain rod above window recess (usually 2-5 inches). See also *Install Curtain Rail* (page 88).

If necessary, cut the curtain rod to the right length with a junior hacksaw.

If you're not attaching the rod to solid brick, locate studs using a detector and attach it to these, if possible. Choose wall anchors, screws, and drill bits to fit your wall. See *Back to Basics* (pages 18-20).

If you're concerned about hidden pipes and cables, use a detector to make sure you don't drill into anything important!

WHAT TO DO

❶ Mark the positions for the end bracket screws (and central, if needed) on the wall in pencil. Check that the marks are level using a long standard level.

❷ Drill at pencil marks to depth of wall anchor, if using, and insert. Screw the brackets in place.

❸ Thread curtain rings or loops onto the curtain rod, secure the rod to the brackets, and leave one ring or loop outside each end bracket. Secure finials to each end of the rod.

HOW TO NAIL IT!

- If hanging heavy curtains, ensure that the screws holding up the rod are long enough to support the weight properly.

- For curtain rods longer than 6 feet, or for heavy curtains, you will need a support bracket in the center as well as at the two ends.

- Remember to check the length of your curtains when deciding on height to place the rod.

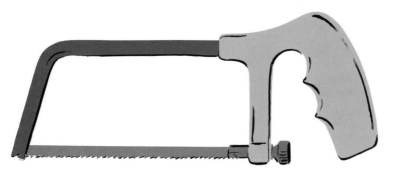

INSTALL CURTAIN RAIL

Although curtain rails can look plain, they are a good solution for tight areas, attaching directly to a window frame, or if you want to use pencil-pleat curtains. Remember to allow for overlap when measuring for your curtains.

▶ YOU'LL NEED

STEEL TAPE MEASURE

CURTAIN RAIL AND HARDWARE (GLIDERS AND HOOKS)

CURTAIN, WITH HEADER TAPE ATTACHED

⚠ **JUNIOR HACKSAW**

MULTIPURPOSE DETECTOR

WORKBENCH OR OTHER SUITABLE CUTTING SURFACE (SEE PAGE 22)

PENCIL

LONG STANDARD LEVEL

⚠ **POWER DRILL, WITH SUITABLE BITS**

SCREWS AND WALL ANCHORS, AS NEEDED

SCREWDRIVER

GETTING STARTED

Choose the position and length of curtain rail. Make sure curtains can be pulled back at least 2 inches from the edge of window to allow for maximum light. Heavy fabric will take up more space.

Choose height of curtain rail above window recess (usually 2-5 inches).

Cut the rail to the right length with a junior hacksaw.

If you're not attaching the rail to solid brick, locate studs using a detector and attach it to these, if possible. Choose wall anchors, screws, and drill bits to fit your wall. See *Back to Basics* (pages 18-20).

If you're concerned about hidden pipes and cables, use a detector to make sure you don't drill into anything important!

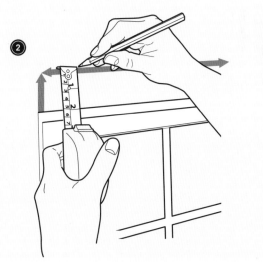

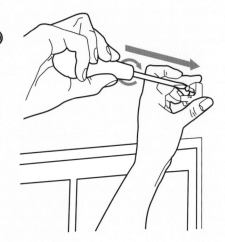

WHAT TO DO

1 Use a pencil and tape measure to mark positions of the brackets, at least 2 inches above the window or window recess. Mark the two side positions first, at 2 inches in from the track ends.

2 Now measure the interim brackets at regular intervals, depending on the width of the window recess and weight of curtain, and always at the same height above the window. Check that the marks are level using a long standard level.

3 Drill into the wall at each bracket mark to depth of wall anchor, if using, and insert. If fixing to studs, drill pilot holes.

4 Screw brackets into position.

5 Attach the stops to the rail ends and click the rail into each bracket.

6 Attach curtain to the rail using gliders and hooks.

HOW TO NAIL IT!

- Use a flexible curtain rail to fit around bay and curved windows.

- If the screws that come with your curtain rail aren't long enough to fit the rail securely to the wall, use longer screws instead.

INSTALL BLINDS

Blinds often provide a sleeker look than curtains and can let in far more light when pulled up. Blackout blinds are great for helping young children stay asleep on very light summer mornings.

YOU'LL NEED

STEEL TAPE MEASURE

BLIND AND HARDWARE

MULTIPURPOSE DETECTOR

PENCIL

LONG STANDARD LEVEL

⚠ POWER DRILL, WITH SUITABLE BITS

SCREWS AND WALL ANCHORS, AS NEEDED

SCREWDRIVER

PLUS, FOR ROLLER BLINDS AND ROLL-UP SHADES:

⚠ JUNIOR HACKSAW

WORKBENCH OR OTHER SUITABLE CUTTING SURFACE (SEE PAGE 22)

SANDPAPER

RULER

UTILITY KNIFE OR SHARP FABRIC SCISSORS

GETTING STARTED

Choose the position for your blind and measure the width and drop length before you go shopping.

For a recessed window, you'll need to be exact about the measurements. Allow for some clearance on either side of the blind and take projecting window handles into account.

You have more flexibility in terms of size if the blind's going on the outside of a recess. Add at least 1 inch on each side to ensure the window is well covered.

If you're not attaching to solid brick, locate studs using a detector and attach the blind to these, if possible. Choose wall anchors, screws, and drill bits to fit your wall. See *Back to Basics* (pages 18–20).

If you're concerned about hidden pipes and cables, use a detector before drilling.

TYPES OF BLINDS

- **Roller blinds** come in different designs and colors, and can add an accent to an otherwise plain room. These blinds can also be cut to size more easily than other types and can be rolled away completely.

- **Roman shades** are great for bringing cosiness to a bedroom. They can be good for blocking out light. Bear in mind that even when open, the fabric will "stack" at the top of the window, reducing visibility but adding color and character.

- **Venetian blinds** can help vary the amount of light in a room during the day. They also allow light in, while maintaining some privacy.

- **Vertical blinds** have a functional look that might remind some people of a doctor's office, but they can work well on sliding or French patio doors and large windows.

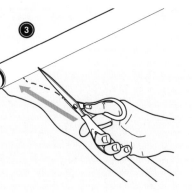

WHAT TO DO

Hang roller blinds

1 Check your measurements once you're back home with the blind and mark the bracket positions in pencil. Use a standard level to check that your marks are level. Allow at least ¼ inch between drill holes and wall edges and corners.

2 To cut the blind down to size, unroll the blind, take out the roller tube (if you can), mark required width on roller tube, and cut through with hacksaw. Sand off rough edges.

3 Mark required width on reverse of roller blind with pencil and ruler; this should be ½ inch shorter than the cut roller tube. Cut out along the line with a utility knife or scissors.

4 Reinsert the roller tube. Fit the control end of blind into the end of the roller tube you want to operate the blind from and fit the dummy end into the other. Push in firmly.

5 Drill holes at your pencilmarks to depth of wall anchor, if using, and push in. If fixing to studs, drill pilot holes. If you find you have a concrete lintel, you will need to use the hammer-action setting on your drill. Screw in the brackets.

6 Slot the blind into the brackets and test it.

Hang Roman and Venetian blinds

Always fit these blinds inside a recess. Follow the instructions for roller blinds, omitting steps 2-4. Your blind should either be made-to-measure, or you should get the best fit possible.

Hang vertical blinds

Always fit into a recess. Follow the instructions for roller blinds, omitting steps 2-4.

HOW TO NAIL IT!

- Looped cords on blinds can be a serious hazard for small children, so make sure the cords are kept well out of reach. You can find safety devices to keep them out of the way of little fingers.

- Open the window to test the location of projecting window handles at their fullest length before you decide where to put up the blind. You may need to move the blind farther away from the window to accommodate it.

INSTALL SHUTTERS

39

Wooden shutters can be a stylish way to shut out light and maximize privacy. Like curtains and blinds, they are installed either inside or outside the window recess. You will need to recruit a helper to lift the frame into position.

▶ YOU'LL NEED

- SHUTTERS AND HARDWARE
- STEEL TAPE MEASURE
- MULTIPURPOSE DETECTOR
- HAMMER
- OLD CARDBOARD
- PENCIL
- SCRATCH AWL OR NAIL
- LONG STANDARD LEVEL
- PAPER AND PEN
- SCREWDRIVER
- ⚠ POWER DRILL, WITH SUITABLE BITS
- SCREWS AND WALL ANCHORS, AS NEEDED
- CAULK AND CAULK GUN

GETTING STARTED

Choose whether your shutters will go inside or outside the window recess and measure accordingly.

For inside mounting, measure at three different heights across window. Note down the smallest width and drop and remove $1/16$ inch to allow space for fitting.

For outside mounting, remember to add the extra space needed for the frame. Refer to the shutter manufacturer for the specifications.

Shutters will need to be made to measure for the best-possible results. When they arrive, the shutter frames will be marked with the window or position they were ordered for, so ensure that the right frames are in the right rooms before you start. They will also come with predrilled holes.

If not attaching to solid brick, locate studs using a detector and attach to these, if possible. Choose wall anchors, screws, and drill bits to fit your wall. See *Back to Basics* (pages 18-20).

If you're concerned about hidden pipes and cables, use a detector before drilling.

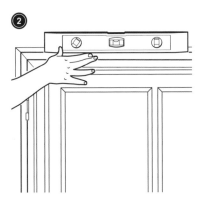

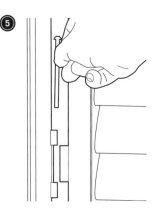

WHAT TO DO

1 Using a hammer, tap supplied fasteners into the frame corners to assemble the shutter frame. Work on top of cardboard to protect the frames.

2 With a helper, lift the frame into position at the window. Mark drill points with scratch awl or nail through the predrilled holes in the frame. Check that they're level with a standard level.

3 Drill all frame holes to depth of wall anchors, if using, and push in. If attaching the frame to studs, drill pilot holes.

4 Attach the frame with just one screw on each side. Do not tighten.

5 Put the panels in the frames by lifting into position and adding the hinge pin to secure. The panels will be labeled with their position from left to right.

6 Once the panels are in, screw in remaining frame screws and tighten.

7 Screw in the remaining screws to attach the frames to the wall. Add any screw caps.

8 Add a line of caulk between the window and shutter frame to finish (see *How to Nail It!*, page 133).

HOW TO NAIL IT!

- For sash windows and inward-opening windows, it's best to attach the shutters outside the recess. It may sound obvious, but shutters can only be inside-mounted if the window recess is deep enough.

- It's really important to get accurate window measurements for your shutters, so use a steel tape measure. Measure once, take a break, then come back and measure again.

- If you have old windows that aren't exactly square, use the smallest measurement in each dimension.

HANG SHEER CURTAINS

Sheer curtains have a terrible reputation for being "twitched" by nosy old neighbors, but when used right, they do a good job of keeping out the busybodies while letting in a good amount of light—and they're very affordable.

YOU'LL NEED

- **SHEER OR VOILE CURTAINS**
- **STEEL TAPE MEASURE**
- **FABRIC SCISSORS**
- **SHEER CURTAIN HEADING TAPE AND SEWING MACHINE, IF NEEDED**
- **LONG STANDARD LEVEL**
- **MULTIPURPOSE DETECTOR, IF NEEDED**
- *TO HANG CURTAINS:*
- **CURTAIN ROD, TRACK, CABLE/WIRE, OR VELCRO TAPE**
- **L-SHAPED SCREW-IN HOOKS, FOR CURTAIN ROD**
- ⚠ **POWER DRILL, WITH SUITABLE BITS, IF NEEDED**
- **WALL ANCHORS, AS NEEDED**
- **HOOKS AND EYES, FOR CURTAIN CABLE**
- **HAMMER AND PLIERS, IF NEEDED**
- **IRON, FOR VELCRO**

GETTING STARTED

Choose to hang your curtains on a rod, track, or cable/wire, or with Velcro.

Ⓐ **Rod:** tension rod stretches across the window recess to hang curtain close to window, allowing room for larger curtains to hang in front, outside the window recess. Very easy to fit.

Ⓑ **Hook and rod:** extending plastic-coated metal rod, useful for hanging curtains above the window recess. Hangs on L-shaped metal screw-in hooks.

Ⓒ **Cable/wire:** fixed with hooks wherever you want. Cheap and easy to fit, but prone to sagging across wider windows.

Ⓓ **Velcro:** easy to fix and keeps the curtains in position.

Sheer and voile curtains sometimes come complete with heading tape that allows you to use regular curtain hooks, or holes to thread a rod through. If not, you may have to add your own (see step 3, opposite).

If fitting screw-in hooks for a rod or wire, and not attaching to solid brick, use a detector to locate studs and attach to these. Choose wall anchors, screws, and drill bits to fit your wall. See *Back to Basics* (pages 18–20).

If you're concerned about hidden pipes and cables, use a detector before any drilling.

WHAT TO DO

❶ Measure window space width and drop, depending on whether you want your curtains inside or outside the recess. For a ruffled look, multiply width by 1.5 (or more) before cutting fabric. If you are mounting the curtains outside the recess, add 2 inches to either side for clearance.

❷ If not supplied as made-to-measure, cut curtains to chosen dimensions.

❸ Hang the curtain:

Rod: thread curtain onto rod, extend rod to fit window width, and twist to fix in place.

Hook and rod: drill holes to depth of wall anchors, if using, and push in. If drilling into studs, drill pilot holes. Screw in L-shaped hooks.

❹ **Net/cable:** mark the height you want the curtains to hang from. Drill holes to depth of wall anchors, if using, and tap curtain-wire hooks in position in the wall. Cut curtain wire to desired length with pliers and thread through heading tape or top hem.

Velcro: cut length to match width of curtain. Iron the soft side of Velcro to the curtain and stick rough edge at desired height on wall or window frame. Stick Velcro together.

HOW TO NAIL IT!

- To get a really neat, bistro look, hem the bottom edge of your sheer curtains and add a second rod or wire to keep them taut.

- Be careful your curtain wire isn't so long that it sags, or too short so that it pulls on the wire hooks.

- If using Velcro tape, choose a color that won't be seen through the curtains.

HANG BLACKOUT CURTAINS

Blackout curtains are great when you want a very dark room for sleeping —but they also muffle sounds from outside and help insulate the room to keep heating bills down.

▶ YOU'LL NEED

BLACKOUT CURTAIN LINING, TO FIT EXISTING CURTAIN SIZE

STANDARD CURTAIN HOOKS

OR, FOR SEPARATE BLACKOUT CURTAINS:

STEEL TAPE MEASURE

BLACKOUT CURTAIN AND HARDWARE, TO FIT MEASUREMENTS

CURTAIN ROD AND HARDWARE OR CURTAIN RAIL AND HARDWARE

MATERIALS FOR ATTACHING CURTAIN ROD OR RAIL (SEE PAGES 87 AND 88)

GETTING STARTED

You can hang a curtain made of blackout fabric—premade ones are available—or add blackout fabric lining to your existing curtains. Where possible, hang the curtain outside the recess, as wide and long as you can for best results.

If you are replacing an existing curtain with a blackout curtain, reuse your curtain rod or rail, but check first that it is strong enough to hold the heavier blackout fabric, and wide enough to allow a minimum of 2 inches each side of the window area to be covered.

WHAT TO DO

Add blackout lining to existing curtains

1 Remove existing curtain and place it face-down on floor or table. Lay blackout lining face-up on top of curtain, lining up the two pleater tapes.

2 Insert curtain hook first into blackout lining tape, then into curtain pleater tape and twist the hook around. Repeat across width of fabrics, so that the two are fastened wrong-sides together.

3 Use curtain hooks to attach the lined curtain back onto curtain rod or rail as before.

Hang separate blackout curtain

1 First measure for curtain dimensions by measuring window recess and adding at least 2 inches on each side and as much as possible above and below.

2 If you need to put up a new curtain rod or rail, see *Install Curtain Rod* (page 87) or *Install Curtain Rail* (page 88).

3 Hang curtain on pole or fit to rail as necessary.

HOW TO NAIL IT!

- Blackout curtains come in all sorts of fabrics, so look around for something that matches your room.

- Remember, the blackout curtain or lining will be visible from the other side of the window, so choose the color carefully if the view from the street is important to you.

- Some blackout curtains come in pairs, with magnetic strips down the middle to help keep them drawn together.

INSTALL DOOR CURTAIN

A heavy curtain hung over an exterior door can be a cosy way of keeping out draughts, but you'll need to consider how you use your door. Think about how often you will be pulling the curtain across to go in and out and whether there is enough clearance for mail to come through a mail slot, if you have one.

▶ YOU'LL NEED

CURTAIN ROD, PORTIÈRE ROD, OR DOOR ROD WITH SWING ARM, PLUS HARDWARE

CURTAIN, TO FIT MEASUREMENTS

STEEL TAPE MEASURE

⚠ JUNIOR HACKSAW, IF NEEDED

WORKBENCH OR OTHER SUITABLE CUTTING SURFACE (SEE PAGE 22), IF NEEDED

PENCIL

LONG STANDARD LEVEL

⚠ POWER DRILL, WITH APPROPRIATE BITS

SCREWS AND WALL ANCHORS, AS NEEDED

GETTING STARTED

Choose whether you want the curtain fixed by a static curtain rod, portière rod, or door rod with swing arm.

Ⓐ Static curtain rod: hanging the curtain above the door recess covers more of the door area and keeps out most draughts, but the pole and curtain will need to be sturdy and securely attached to withstand all the pulling and moving each time you go through the door.

Ⓑ Portière rod: designed to fit onto the door so that the curtain moves with the door when it opens. Convenient for an often-used door, but since the curtain only extends a little way past the door edges, it's less effective at keeping out all the draughts.

Ⓒ Door rod with swing arm: attached to the wall at just one end, the rod and curtain can swing with the door as it opens, and stay "parked" in an open or closed position. Suitable for light-weight or medium-weight fabrics only.

If not attaching to solid brick, locate studs using a detector and choose wall anchors, screws, and drill bits to fit your wall. See *Back to Basics* (page 18–20).

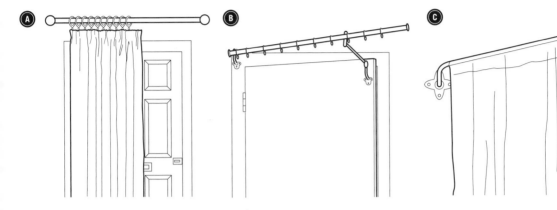

WHAT TO DO

① Measure the space to determine the curtain's dimensions and length of rod or rail required. Ensure that the rod or rail is at least 2 inches above the door and long enough to allow the curtain to be pulled completely back to one side without obstructing the door. If necessary, cut the rod or rail to the right length with a junior hacksaw.

② Mark chosen positions for hardware using pencil and standard level.

③ Drill holes as necessary. Refer to manufacturer's instructions, fitting wall anchors, if needed, and screws where attaching brackets to wall.

④ Thread the curtain onto rod, or attach to rings or hooks and hang it up. Attach any finials or curtain stops

• Door curtains need to be fairly heavy, so make sure the supporting rod is sturdy and well secured with long-enough screws and suitable wall anchors.

HANG CURTAIN AS ROOM DIVIDER

Curtains are a flexible way of dividing rooms, especially to make one area seem cosier, or to zone off open-plan living spaces. You can hang a lightweight curtain across a wide area using a high-tension wire. To hang a heavier dividing curtain over a shorter distance, see *Install Door Curtain* (page 98).

▶ YOU'LL NEED

STEEL TAPE MEASURE

MULTIPURPOSE DETECTOR

PENCIL

⚠ POWER DRILL, WITH SUITABLE BITS

SCREW-IN HOOKS WITH ANCHORS (THESE LOOK LIKE THEY HAVE A WALL ANCHOR ATTACHED)

STEEL HANGING WIRE, TO FIT MEASUREMENTS, PLUS 20 INCHES EXTRA

2 TURNBUCKLES

APPROX 6 WIRE ROPE CLIPS, TO FIT WIRE

CURTAIN, TO FIT MEASUREMENTS

WIRE CUTTERS

GETTING STARTED

To ensure that you buy the correct size curtains, measure the distance across the room where you want the curtain to hang, and measure the drop height. Multiply the width by 1.5 or more to allow the curtain to gather nicely across the space.

If not attaching to solid brick, choose wall anchors, screws, and drill bits to fit your wall. See *Back to Basics* (pages 18–20).

If you are worried about hidden pipes or cables, use a detector before drilling, or a multipurpose one if you also want to locate studs (see page 21). It can be useful to attach the hooks to studs, especially if using heavy fabric.

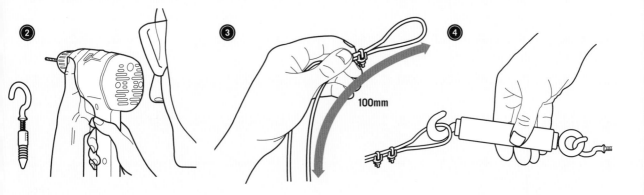

WHAT TO DO

① Using a pencil, mark positions for hooks on each wall. Measure carefully to ensure that they are at the same height.

② Drill holes at markings and tap in screw-in hooks with anchors.

③ Make a loop at one end of wire, with at least 4 inches of spare wire held alongside length. Place wire rope clips along loop at intervals to secure.

④ Unscrew the turnbuckle to expand it, insert the eye end into hook and the wire loop into other end of turnbuckle.

⑤ Stretch wire to other side of room and thread the curtain onto the wire.

⑥ Pull wire taut and repeat turnbuckle attachment at other end of cable. Use wire cutters to cut off any excess.

⑦ Turn turnbuckles at either end to fine-tune the tautness.

HOW TO NAIL IT!

- A quick and easy way of adding a lightweight curtain to an empty doorway, between rooms, is to drill two holes 2 inches above the doorframe, 2 inches out from each corner. Insert wall anchors, if needed, and screw in two hooks. Thread the curtain onto a lightweight rod—a long dowel would also work well—and place it on the hooks.

- If you want to hang very heavy curtains, use a rod that's attached all the way along to distribute the weight.

INSTALL DECORATIVE WINDOW FILM

44

If you have glass doors or windows with an ugly view, or facing a busy street, window film is an affordable alternative to frosted glass panels. Try a simple frosted look or opt for a more decorative pattern.

▶ YOU'LL NEED

SPRAY BOTTLE WITH SOAP SOLUTION (2 FL OZ DISHWASHING LIQUID TO 1 QUART WARM WATER)

SQUEEGEE

WINDOW SCRAPER

LINT-FREE CLOTH

STEEL TAPE MEASURE

PENCIL AND RULER

WINDOW FILM

SCISSORS

STRAIGHTEDGE

UTILITY KNIFE

GETTING STARTED

Clean the window with the soap solution and squeegee until all grease and dust are removed. Dry with a lint-free cloth.

Measure dimensions to be covered by the film and add 1 inch in each direction. Mark lightly on backing paper with pencil and ruler. Cut out the film with scissors.

WHAT TO DO

1. Wet the window with soap solution using fine spray. Ensure glass is covered.

2. Place film onto the glass with the adhesive side facing you.

3. Peel off liner and spray adhesive side liberally with soap solution.

4. Without allowing the film to curl, reverse the film so that the adhesive side is against window, with a little film overlapping window edges on all sides. Slide film until position is accurate.

5. If any dirt is caught under film, peel back, remove with scraper, re-wet, and reapply.

6. Once in position, smooth out film using palm of your hand, in a swooping motion from the center out. Repeat using a squeegee, carefully moving all the liquid from underneath. This is easier to do if the surface is wet.

7. Slide straightedge against each window edge and use as a guide to cut off excess film with utility knife.

8. Repeat step 6 to strengthen the bond, wetting the film surface again to help squeegee to move.

9. Leave to dry for two days before touching.

HOW TO NAIL IT!

- If any of the window isn't wet when you apply the film, it will stick to the dry areas, allowing air bubbles to get in.

- If covering large windows, call in another pair of hands to help you keep the film straight while turning it around.

FLOORS AND WALLS

EVERYTHING
YOU NEED
TO GET THE
JOB DONE

PATCH CARPET

If your carpet has a scorch mark, burn, stain, or worn area that can't be hidden by furniture, you can patch it if you can find a piece of matching carpet. The job is easier if you're dealing with plain carpet, but with care, you can still do a good job on patterned ones.

YOU'LL NEED

SPARE CARPET
UTILITY KNIFE
⚠ **CARPET ADHESIVE**
VACUUM CLEANER

GETTING STARTED

Find the spare carpet for the replacement patch. Ideally, you'll have leftover scraps from fitting the carpet, but if not, ask the supplier for a matching remnant. In the worst-case scenario, you could take a piece from under or behind a piece of never-moved furniture.

WHAT TO DO

1 Cut out damaged area using a utility knife with a sharp blade. Be careful to leave carpet padding intact.

2 Use cut-out piece as a template to cut out a new patch from spare carpet. Be careful to align pile direction and any patterning before cutting.

3 Spread carpet adhesive on back of replacement patch and on edges surrounding the hole.

4 Press replacement patch into the hole and use fingers to roughen up the pile.

5 Leave six hours to dry, then vacuum the patched area.

HOW TO NAIL IT!

• If you accidentally cut through the padding, tape it up with heavy-duty carpet tape.

INSTALL CARPET AND PADDING

A cheap carpet, well laid, can look fabulous. An expensive carpet laid badly will always look terrible. If you're laying a carpet for the first time, start with a small room, if possible. You can rent the necessary equipment from a large hardware store or tool rental company.

▶ YOU'LL NEED

MATERIALS FOR PREPARING FLOOR (SEE *GETTING STARTED*)

STEEL TAPE MEASURE

CARPET, TO FIT SPACE, PLUS EXTRA

CARPET PADDING, TO FIT SPACE, PLUS EXTRA

MULTIPURPOSE DETECTOR

PENCIL

HEAVY-DUTY GLOVES

KNEEPADS (OPTIONAL)

CARPET TACK STRIPS FOR PERIMETER OF ROOM, EXCLUDING DOORWAYS

⚠ SMALL HANDSAW OR BACK SAW

WORKBENCH OR OTHER SUITABLE CUTTING SURFACE (SEE PAGE 22)

⚠ GRAB ADHESIVE, IF NEEDED

HAMMER

DOOR THRESHOLD, WITH HARDWARE

⚠ POWER DRILL, WITH SUITABLE BIT

SCREWDRIVER

LINING PAPER, TO FIT SPACE

CARPET TACKS, STAPLE GUN, OR SPRAY ADHESIVE

⚠ HEAVY-DUTY UTILITY KNIFE OR CARPET KNIFE

CARPET TAPE

CARPET KNEE KICKER AND CARPET TUCKER

GETTING STARTED

Remove old carpet, vinyl, or other floor coverings and ensure that the surface is dry, firm, and level. If laying over concrete, test for moisture. See *Install Laminate Flooring* (page 110).

Carpets should always be fitted with padding to help them last longer and feel more comfortable. Fit the best quality you can afford: hessian- or woven-backed carpets are generally better quality than foam-backed carpets.

Measure the room. When ordering carpet and padding, add about 4 inches in each direction to allow for cutting to exact size. Include alcoves and halfway into any doorways.

Use a multipurpose detector to locate any hidden pipes and cables under the floor; mark the positions in pencil. In these places you'll need to attach the tack strips with adhesive instead of nails.

WHAT TO DO

① Fit tack strips around the edge of the room

A Wear heavy-duty gloves and kneepads and cut tack strips to length using a saw.

B Position with angled edge facing baseboard (teeth pointing to wall) and lengths butted together. Leave ¼-inch gap between tack strip and baseboard. If you have a curved area, cut the tack strip into small pieces to follow the curve. If the tack strip can't be nailed, apply grab adhesive and press in place.

C Use hammer to secure rest of tack strips in place, being careful not to damage any baseboards.

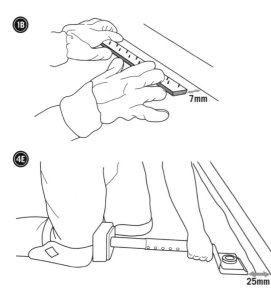

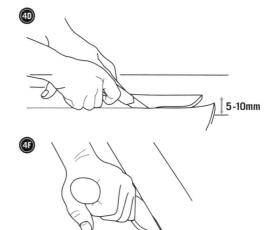

2 Install door threshold

At doorway, check for hidden pipes and cables, then drill holes to secure threshold bar to floor with screws.

3 Lay carpet padding

A Roll out paper lining to cover space, butting up to tack strips and overlapping strips by around 1 inch. Secure with tacks, staples, or adhesive.

B Loosely lay padding on floor, rubber-side down. Use utility knife to cut padding flush with tack strips. Butt up different sections of padding and secure with carpet tape. The padding should be as smooth and level as possible so don't overlap any sections.

4 Lay carpet

A Roll carpet out loosely into position, leaving 2–4 inches excess at each edge.

B At internal corners, cut triangular notches out of spare carpet to help it lie flat. At external corners, cut a slit down from the edge. In both cases, leave around 4 inches of excess. See *Install Vinyl Flooring*, steps 3 and 4 (page 113).

C Work one wall at a time. Starting at end of longest wall and working backwards towards the doorway, crease carpet firmly against baseboard using a carpet tucker. This will make a fold line for cutting.

D Cut along carpet edge with heavy-duty utility knife or carpet knife leaving $^{3}/_{16} - ^{3}/_{8}$ inch excess. Be careful not to damage the baseboard.

E Use carpet knee kicker to hook carpet onto tack strips: place the stretcher, teeth-down, about 1 inch from baseboard and push against the padded end with your knee.

F In this position, use carpet tucker to push excess down between baseboard and tack strip.

G Repeat steps C–F, moving across the room to fit carpet up to wall opposite the one you've just done. Finish with adjacent walls. At door threshold push carpet edge underneath bar with screwdriver.

HOW TO NAIL IT!

- Carpet looks best with the pile facing away from the window. Rub your hand over the carpet: one way will feel smooth and the other will feel rough. The carpet should feel smooth when running your hand away from the window.

- If your carpet has a pattern, stand in the doorway to check it looks square in the room before you fix it in place.

- Some carpets come with an integral padding. In this case, skip the carpet padding stage, but don't forget to lay lining paper first.

INSTALL NATURAL FLOORING

47

There's now a large range of floor coverings made from natural fibers, which are more ecologically friendly than synthetic carpet and are often woven by hand into interesting patterns and textures. Be warned, though: These are not the easiest carpets to clean.

▶ YOU'LL NEED

MATERIALS FOR PREPARING FLOOR (SEE *GETTING STARTED*)

STEEL TAPE MEASURE

FLOORING, TO FIT SPACE, PLUS EXTRA

KNEEPADS (OPTIONAL)

CARPET TACK STRIPS (WITH NO PINS, OR VERY SHORT ONES)

MULTIPURPOSE DETECTOR

⚠ POWER DRILL, WITH SUITABLE BIT

DOOR THRESHOLD, WITH HARDWARE

CARPET ADHESIVE

NOTCHED TROWEL

⚠ HEAVY-DUTY UTILITY KNIFE OR CARPET KNIFE

CARPET TUCKER

SCREWDRIVER

GETTING STARTED

Remove old carpet, vinyl, or other floor coverings and ensure the surface is dry, firm, and level. If you have a concrete floor, test for moisture. See *Install Laminate Flooring* (page 110).

Measure the room to be covered by multiplying its length by its width. Allow around 4 inches excess at each edge. Include alcoves and halfway into any doorways.

Unroll the natural floor covering in the room it will fill and leave it to acclimatize for 24-48 hours before laying. If you can't lay it out completely, loosely unroll the carpet.

Make sure the room you are working in is well ventilated. This job can be hard on the knees, so kneepads are useful.

TYPES OF NATURAL FLOORING

Coir fibers come from coconut husks. They are extracted by hand, softened in seawater, and woven into flooring that is durable and good value. It stains easily, however, so spray with protective coating.

Jute fibers are extracted from the stalks of giant corchorus plants that grow in the tropics. The fibers are fine and soft underfoot, so jute flooring is well suited to bedrooms, but not durable enough for elsewhere. Jute has a "tweedy" look.

Seagrass grows in tropical meadows and on riverbanks. The fibers are extracted by hand, dried, and spun, before being woven. Seagrass is very durable, but it retains moisture, so isn't suitable for bathrooms and kitchens.

Sisal fibers come from an agave plant. The fibers make durable flooring suitable for hallways and stairs. They are easily dyed, so can come in a range of colors.

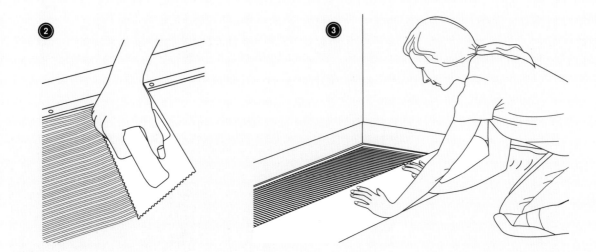

WHAT TO DO

1 Fit tack strips to perimeter of room. At doorway, check for hidden pipes and cables, then drill holes to secure threshold bar to floor with screws.

2 Spread carpet adhesive over first third of floor using notched trowel, starting at wall edge furthest from door.

3 Unroll carpet onto the adhesive, leaving about 4 inches excess at floor edges and pressing as you go to ensure complete coverage.

4 Repeat for next third of the floor, and again until floor is covered.

5 Remove any excess by running utility knife or carpet knife around edge of wall, leaving around 2 inches extra. Be very careful not to mark the baseboards. At doorway, cut to line up with door threshold bar.

6 Tuck carpet edge behind tack strips using carpet tucker. See *Install Carpet and Padding*, step 4F (page 107). At doorway, tuck flooring underneath door threshold with a screwdriver.

7 Leave flooring for at least 24 hours before moving furniture into room. Check manufacturer's instructions for timings.

HOW TO NAIL IT!

- Ensure the carpet adhesive you use has a low water content. Natural fibers absorb moisture so should be kept away from it as much as possible.

- Be generous with adhesive; the textured backing of the carpet takes a lot to be completely covered. Without enough adhesive the carpet won't bond properly to the floor and it may shrink.

- When cutting the carpet at room edges, try to follow straight lines along the weave, rather than cutting across weave patterns.

INSTALL LAMINATE FLOORING

Laminate flooring is hard-wearing, easy to clean, and easy to install. You don't have to spend much to get a really professional look. This job can be very hard on the knees, however, so kneepads are useful.

▶ YOU'LL NEED

MATERIALS FOR PREPARING FLOOR (SEE *GETTING STARTED*)

STEEL TAPE MEASURE

LAMINATE FLOORING, TO COVER FLOOR SPACE, PLUS EXTRA

MATCHING FLOORING TRIM, TO COVER PERIMETER, PLUS EXTRA

UNDERLAYMENT FOR LAMINATE FLOORS

SCISSORS OR UTILITY KNIFE

TAPE

⚡ **TOOL UP** JIGSAW

⚡ **TOOL DOWN** JUNIOR HACKSAW

WORKBENCH OR OTHER SUITABLE CUTTING SURFACE (SEE PAGE 22)

EXPANSION SPACERS, PENCIL

⚠ GRAB ADHESIVE

HAMMER AND FINISH NAILS OR HEAVY BOOKS

GETTING STARTED

Remove old carpet, vinyl, or other floor coverings and ensure that the surface is dry, firm, and level. You can lay laminate on top of ceramic or vinyl tiles if you don't want to remove them first.

If you're laying the flooring on top of concrete, check the surface for moisture by taping one square yard of plastic sheeting onto the concrete floor; tape all edges down and leave overnight. If any condensation has appeared, consult a waterproofing specialist.

Calculate how many packs of laminate flooring you'll need. Measure the room width and length at widest points, then multiply to calculate surface area. Add extra for wastage. Divide this total by the surface area provided by each pack. Round up to the nearest whole number.

Next, measure the perimeter of the room to calculate the amount of flooring trim needed and buy ten percent extra.

Allow the laminate floorboards to acclimatize by leaving them for 48 hours in the room they will cover, before laying.

Decide in which direction to lay the floorboards:

- Running floorboards lengthwise, towards a light source, is the most forgiving for visible joints. It will also make a room feel longer.

- Running floorboards across the width of the room will make it feel wider.

- If laying laminate over a wooden floor, lay the boards at 90 degrees to the floorboards below for the strongest result.

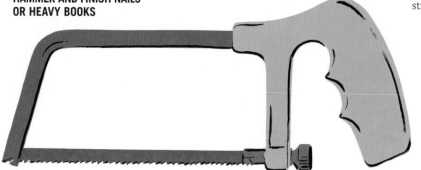

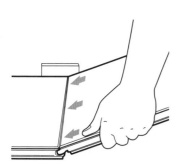

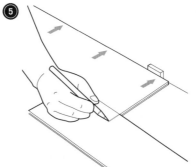

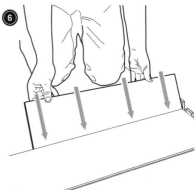

WHAT TO DO

1 Roll out underlayment over the entire floor. Trim to fit with scissors or a utility knife. Tape joins securely, with no overlap.

2 Loosely lay out the first row of boards, end to end, to ensure there won't be a very short strip at one end. If the last board will need to be cut to less than one-third of its length, cut the first board to less than a full length so that neither board is too short. Repeat this process for the width of the room to ensure neither first nor last board is too narrow.

3 Lay the first board in the corner, with an expansion spacer between it and the wall on both edges. Expansion spacers allow for natural movement of the boards, and should be placed wherever the boards meet the wall.

4 Fit the next board end-on, slotting the tongue into the groove at a 30-degree angle. Lower the board to lock into place.

5 Continue along the row until you need to cut. Turn the end board around so that the tongue-end is against wall and positioned alongside penultimate board. Mark a line on the end board at level of penultimate board.

6 If the offcut is more than 12 inches long, use it to start the next row. If not, cut another board in half and start laying the second row next to where you started the first. With the cut end against the wall, angle the new board against the first board with tongue in groove. Click down to lock in place. Repeat along the row.

7 To finish, remove expansion spacers and add matching trim, cutting miters at corners. Measure and cut lengths of trim and/or shoe molding and glue to wall or baseboard—not the floor. Press in place and hold firm by hammering in finish nails, or place heavy books on top, until dry.

HOW TO NAIL IT!

- **Choose a combined underlayment and waterproofing membrane if you are at all worried about moisture.**

- **If you have an uneven floor, choose a thick underlayment such as wood fiber. This will also insulate for sound and heat. You can add a waterproofing membrane underneath, if necessary.**

- **Cut boards outside or in another room, if possible, to avoid dust getting into the underlayment.**

INSTALL VINYL FLOORING

49

Vinyl flooring is durable and comes in all sorts of colors and designs. It is much easier to clean than carpet and is ideal for areas that are exposed to a lot of moisture, such as bathrooms.

▶ YOU'LL NEED

MATERIALS FOR PREPARING FLOOR (SEE *GETTING STARTED*)

STEEL TAPE MEASURE

ROLL OF VINYL FLOORING, TO FIT SPACE, PLUS EXTRA

SCISSORS

SOFT BROOM

STEEL STRAIGHTEDGE OR RULER

UTILITY KNIFE

SMALL BLOCK OF WOOD

⚠ VINYL SPRAY ADHESIVE AND MASK

⬆ **TOOL UP** FLOOR ROLLER

⬇ **TOOL DOWN** ROLLING PIN OR CLEAN PAINT ROLLER

PIPE-AND-CABLE DETECTOR

⚠ POWER DRILL, WITH APPROPRIATE BIT

DOOR THRESHOLD, WITH HARDWARE

SCREWDRIVER

GETTING STARTED

Remove old carpet, vinyl, or other floor coverings and ensure surface is dry, firm, and level.

Timber subfloor: put down 1-inch exterior-grade plywood, to take out any ridges. Screw into boards below at 12-inch intervals. Fill and sand any joins to ensure that the surface is perfectly smooth.

Concrete subfloor: if you have a concrete floor, test for moisture. See *Install Laminate Flooring* (page 110). If laying over bumpy concrete or tiles, you can use a self-leveling compound to achieve a smooth base. Basically,

over time, bumps show through vinyl so it's best to get your floor as smooth as possible. Once the floor is flat, paint primer on any porous surface such as cement, plywood, hardboard, or particle board, before you begin.

Measure the room to be covered by multiplying its length by its width. Add about 4 inches to measurements at each edge. Include alcoves and halfway into any doorways.

Vinyl sheets come in different widths, so choose one that will cover the whole floor, or that will do it in a sensible number of strips. Calculate how many you will need by measuring the length of longest wall and dividing by width of roll. Measure adjacent wall and multiply by number of strips to determine the length needed.

Leave vinyl in room for 48 hours to acclimatize. In cold weather, put the heating on to prevent it from becoming brittle.

The method you use for securing the vinyl will vary. Some vinyls come with peel-off adhesive, some only require sticking at doorways, seams, and edges; and some require no gluing. If using adhesive, consult manufacturer's recommendations.

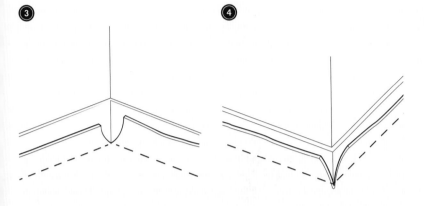

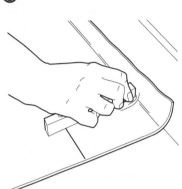

WHAT TO DO

1 Take off your shoes to avoid treading grit into the underside of vinyl.

2 Unroll vinyl face-up against longest continuous wall. Using scissors, roughly cut edge down to leave an excess of about 4 inches against baseboards. You can trim more precisely once it is all in place.

3 At internal corners, cut triangular notches out of "spare" vinyl to help sheet lie flat.

4 At external corners, make a straight cut down from vinyl edge to floor level.

5 Use soft broom to brush surface, removing air pockets.

6 Where more than one piece of vinyl is required, fit largest piece first, then lay next rough-cut piece so that it overlaps the first by 1⅓– 2 inches. To cut seam, place straightedge or ruler with guiding edge alongside edge of lower piece of vinyl. Hold firmly and cut through both layers with utility knife. Go slowly and do not attempt it in one stroke! Remove cut strip.

7 Press vinyl sheet against base of baseboards or wall using small block of wood to help crease.

8 Hold sheet hard to baseboard with metal straightedge and cut along crease with sharp utility knife. Move knife carefully, removing waste frequently to check that the cut is accurate.

9 To fix with adhesive, roll back 50 percent of vinyl. Wear mask and apply glue to floor. Press vinyl firmly and slowly onto adhesive to ensure a good bond. Use a rolling motion to reduce air bubbles and follow with a floor roller, rolling pin, or clean paint roller. Roll from the center of the floor out, with firm pressure. Repeat with other half of vinyl. Roll again between one and four hours later.

10 At doorway, cut vinyl to line up with flooring in next room. Check for hidden pipes and cables, then drill holes to secure threshold bar to floor with screws. Push vinyl edge underneath with screwdriver.

11 Avoid walking on floor for at least 24 hours after installation. Check manufacturer's instructions for timings.

HOW TO NAIL IT!

- If you're using vinyl flooring on kitchen or bathroom floors, seal the edges with silicone caulk to make a waterproof barrier. See *Apply Silicone Caulk* (page 46).

- Try to avoid joining strips of vinyl in doorways or areas of heavy wear.

- To lay around a curve, make a paper template. Take a piece of paper (wider than the curved object) and cut slits ⅓–⅔ inch wide along one edge. Place paper with slits up against curve, crease slits against curve, and draw pencil line around crease. Remove paper and cut along curved line. Place template on vinyl and draw around line. Using sharp utility knife or scissors, cut, check, and trim for a perfect fit.

INSTALL VINYL TILES

Laying soft vinyl tiles is easier than laying vinyl sheeting. If you make a mistake, you've only wasted one tile, not a whole sheet. The first tile to be laid is called the key tile; find a helper and take time to get its position right. You can buy self-adhesive tiles if you prefer.

▶ YOU'LL NEED

- **MATERIALS FOR PREPARING FLOOR (SEE *GETTING STARTED*)**
- **STEEL TAPE MEASURE**
- **SOFT VINYL TILES, TO FIT SPACE, PLUS EXTRA**
- **PENCIL OR CHALK**
- **CHALK LINE**
- **STRING**
- **CHINA MARKER OR ORDINARY PENCIL**
- **CUTTING BOARD OR SCRAP HARDBOARD**
- **UTILITY KNIFE**
- **STRAIGHTEDGE**
- *FOR NON-ADHESIVE TILES:*
- ⚠ **TILE ADHESIVE**
- **NOTCHED TROWEL**
- **SMALL ROLLER**
- **DAMP CLOTH OR SPONGE**

GETTING STARTED

Remove old carpet, vinyl, or other floor coverings and ensure surface is dry, firm, and level.

Timber floor: you will need to put down 1-inch exterior-grade plywood first, to take out the ridges. Screw into boards below at 12-inch intervals. Fill and sand any joins to ensure that the surface is perfectly smooth.

Concrete and tiles: if you have a concrete floor, test for moisture. See *Install Laminate Flooring* (page 110). If laying over bumpy concrete or tiles, you can use a self-leveling compound to achieve a smooth base. Basically, over time, bumps show through vinyl so try to get your floor as smooth as possible.

Once the floor is flat, paint primer on any porous surface such as cement, plywood, hardboard, or particle board, before you begin.

Measure area to be tiled. Measure tiles and calculate number of tiles needed for the area. See *Tile Wall* (page 38).

Check that all the packs of tiles list the same batch or item numbers, or you may find they have color differences.

Leave the tiles in the room they will cover for 24 hours to acclimatize.

To get the best symmetrical results, tile from the center out.

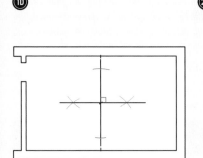

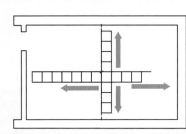

WHAT TO DO

1 Find center of room

A Measure one wall, find its midpoint, and mark it on the floor in pencil. Repeat on opposite wall and stretch a chalk line between the two points.

B Mark midpoint of this line. Attach pencil or chalk to one yard of string. With one person holding the string end at the midpoint, draw semicircles at two intersections with chalk line.

C Move end of string to intersection of points and draw two semicircles towards center of room, at either side of chalk line. Repeat at other mark so you have two crosses where the semicircles intersect.

D Make chalk line between two intersection points. The cross-point will be a perfect right angle in center of room.

2 Lay tiles

A Without sticking, loosely lay out a test row of tiles starting at the center line and working towards the wall. If the last tile would be cut too narrow, move start tile back half a tile-width and repeat test row. Adding onto initial row, lay test rows towards other walls, adjusting start positions so each row ends with at least half a tile. Mark final start position for key tile on floor with pencil or chalk.

B *For self-adhesive tiles:* peel backing paper off first tile and press down in start position, as above.

For non-adhesive tiles: spread tile adhesive over floor with notched trowel, covering an area of one square yard at a time. Make sure you can still see chalk lines for starting position. Press first tile into adhesive so each part of it is in contact.

C Lay second tile on other side of chalk line butting up to first tile. Lay first four tiles in a square of tiles, then continue until half the room is tiled. Don't fill edge gaps until the end.

D *For non-adhesive tiles:* use a small roller to ensure that all tiles are well stuck down, paying attention to edges. Wipe away any adhesive that comes through joins with damp cloth or sponge.

3 Cut and lay tiles for gaps at baseboards

A Place tile to be cut exactly on top of last full tile. Place a second tile on top with its edge butting up to wall. Mark along edge of top tile onto face of tile below using china marker or ordinary pencil. See *Install Ceramic Floor Tiles, step 3A* (page 117).

B On cutting board or scrap board, cut partway through marked line using utility knife and straightedge. Break tile along score mark by bending until it snaps. See also *Cut Tiles* (page 36).

C Check fit of cut tile before sticking it in place.

HOW TO NAIL IT!

- When calculating number of tile packs to buy, always round up and err on the side of caution. Some tiles will be wasted.

- Once tiles are laid, leave floor for at least 24 hours before walking on it. Check the manufacturer's instructions for timings.

INSTALL CERAMIC FLOOR TILES

51

Ceramic tiles are hard-wearing, easy to clean, and resistant to spills and stains. They are expensive, though, so take extra care when laying them. Ask your local hardware store for advice on choosing the right grout for your tiles.

▶ YOU'LL NEED

MATERIALS FOR PREPARING FLOOR (SEE *GETTING STARTED*)

STEEL TAPE MEASURE

TILES TO FILL SPACE, PLUS EXTRA

PENCIL, CHALK LINE, AND STRING

▲ TILE ADHESIVE

NOTCHED TROWEL

◆ **TOOL UP** TILE SPACERS

▼ **TOOL DOWN** MATCHES

STANDARD LEVEL, TROWEL

CHINA MARKER

↕ **TOOL UP** TILE CUTTER FOR STRAIGHT CUTS; JIGSAW, WITH TILE-CUTTING BLADE, PLUS CLAMP, FOR SHAPED CUTS

↕ **TOOL DOWN** TILE SCORER FOR STRAIGHT CUTS; TILE SAW AND CLAMP, OR TILE NIPPERS, FOR SHAPED CUTS

SANDPAPER OR TILE FILE

CERAMIC TILE SEALER (IF LAYING NATURAL OR POROUS TILES)

FLOOR TILE GROUT (PREMIXED OR POWDERED)

RUBBER GLOVES (OPTIONAL)

DOWEL

SPONGE AND CLOTHS

FLEXIBLE CAULK, IN SAME COLOR AS GROUT, AND CAULK GUN

GETTING STARTED

Prepare the existing floor.

Concrete floor: clean with detergent and water. Ensure it is thoroughly dry.

Timber floor: strengthen by laying 1-inch exterior-grade plywood. Screw into boards below at 12-inch intervals.

Ceramic/quarry tiles: check that all tiles are securely stuck down and clean.

Vinyl flooring: check that all tiles are securely stuck down and clean.

Measure the area to be tiled. Measure tiles and calculate the number of tiles needed for the area. See *Tile Wall* (page 38).

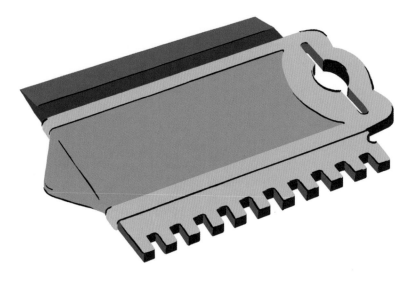

2D

3A

WHAT TO DO

1 Find center of room, then locate best position for key tile. See *Install Vinyl Tiles*, step 1 (page 115).

2 **Lay tiles**

A Cover about one square yard of floor at a time with adhesive, using notched trowel. Make sure you can still see chalk lines for starting position.

B Lay first key tile, giving it a slight twist to bed it into adhesive properly.

C Work a single row out towards one wall, fitting spacers or matches to keep tiles evenly spaced. Use standard level to check tiles are level.

D Lay next row at a right angle out from key tile towards wall, then work one row at a time to fill this quarter of the room.

E Repeat process, filling a quarter of the room at a time, until all but cut tiles at edges are laid.

F Use trowel to clean out adhesive in gaps around the walls before it sets. Leave tiles for 24 hours before cutting and laying edge tiles.

3 **Cut and lay tiles for gaps at baseboards**

A Place tile to be cut exactly on top of last full tile. Place a third tile on top with its edge butting up to wall. Mark along edge of top tile onto face of tile below using china marker.

B Cut just short of marked line to allow space for grout. See *Cut Tiles* (page 36).

C Apply adhesive to back of each cut tile and lay in place. Leave for 24 hours.

4 **Grout tiles**

A If your tiles are natural stone or very porous, apply tile sealer before and after grouting.

B When adhesive has set, if using powdered grout, mix it to a fairly dry consistency. Get advice from tile retailer for consistency needed. See *Grout Tiles* (page 34). Leave for a few minutes to stand. A dry grout mix needs to be applied carefully with fingers to prevent staining of tile surface. Wear rubber gloves, if you prefer. If tiles are glazed, pour grout mix over tiles and spread with rubber edge of spreader.

C As grout starts to set, press and smooth it into joints with dowel or finger, to create neat concave line. Compacting it like this makes it water-resistant. Wipe off excess grout with a damp sponge.

D Leave grout to harden for one hour. Wipe with damp cloth, then polish with dry cloth.

E Seal edge of floor with flexible caulk.

F Leave floor for at least 24 hours before walking on, and at least 48 hours before using it heavily.

HOW TO NAIL IT!

- Because freshly laid tiles have to be left untouched for 48 hours, don't find yourself unable to use the kitchen. Tile half a room at a time before taking a long break and make sure you leave an exit path so you don't have to tread on any tiles.

- Push tile spacers well below the surface of the tile so that they won't protrude through the grout at the end.

- A short length of hose works well to smooth and shape grout.

REPAIR SCRATCHES IN FLOORBOARDS

52

The best way to get an even wooden floor is by sanding, but if you just have a few scratches, small holes, or gaps, they can be repaired without embarking on such a big job.

YOU'LL NEED

- **FLOOR OR MULTISURFACE CLEANER AND SOFT CLOTHS**
- **STEEL WOOL**
- **FINE-GRADE SANDPAPER**
- ⚠ **MINERAL SPIRITS**
- **PUTTY KNIFE**
- **WOOD FILLER OR PUTTY, TO MATCH FLOOR COLOR**
- **MATERIALS FOR VARNISHING FLOOR (SEE PAGE 127)**

GETTING STARTED

Determine how deep your scratch is. Light scratches can be dealt with using steel wool, but deeper scratches will need fine-grade sandpaper.

WHAT TO DO

❶ Clean the area with floor or multi-surface cleaner.

❷ Rub over scratch with steel wool or fine-grade sandpaper, taking care to go in direction of wood grain and only over scratch.

❸ Clean and smooth the area with mineral spirits on a soft cloth.

❹ Use putty knife to press wood filler into scratched area. Leave to dry.

❺ Sand excess dried filler to the level of the wood, using fine-grade sandpaper. Clean away dust.

❻ Revarnish repaired area to match the rest of the floor. See *Varnish Floorboards* (page 127).

HOW TO NAIL IT!

- If you have recently sanded your floor, salvage the sawdust from the sander, mix with wood glue, and use to fill small holes in the wood.

- Always sand along the grain of the wood or you risk damaging it further.

FIX CREAKING FLOORBOARDS

Floorboards can creak either because their fastening screws have come loose, or because they've swollen and now rub against each other. Once you've found the problem, it's easy to fix. If a floorboard covers an area of pipes or cables, fixing it with a screw instead of a nail will allow easy access.

▶ YOU'LL NEED

- TALCUM POWDER
- OLD KNIFE
- PLIERS OR CLAW HAMMER
- WIDE-BLADED CHISEL, IF NEEDED
- 2¼-INCH SCREWS
- ⚠ POWER DRILL, WITH COUNTERSINK BIT
- SCREWDRIVER
- FLOORBOARD NAILS

GETTING STARTED

Remove any floor coverings and press on the boards with your feet to pinpoint the problem place. Sprinkle talcum powder along the cracks and work in with a knife. This may be enough to solve the problem.

If the floorboard still creaks, you will need to screw it down or nail it to secure and stop the movement. You can screw directly into existing nail holes if they're in good condition.

WHAT TO DO

1 Use existing nail holes

A Prize out old nails with pliers or claw hammer; if you need to lift board slightly to pull nails higher, drive a wide-bladed chisel between the boards and prize up a little. Push board back down, leaving nails slightly raised, and remove.

B Screw in 2¼ inch screws and secure tightly. If screw heads sit slightly above the surface, remove, countersink (see *Back to Basics*, page 18), and screw back in.

2 Use new nail holes

Drive nails in away from old holes but near enough so you go into joist underneath. If in doubt, prize up board as above, and take a look, marking the position of the joist on floorboard.

If you are driving nails near the very end of board, drill small pilot holes (smaller than width of your nail) first, to prevent the board from splitting.

HOW TO NAIL IT!

- If board end doesn't fix to joist, screw a 1 x 2-inch batten onto nearest joist end to provide an anchor for the board.

FILL FLOORBOARD GAPS

54

As good as stripped floorboards look, the gaps between them can let cold air circulate. Stop the draughts by sealing up the gaps. The amount you'll save on heating bills will pay for the job within a year.

▶ YOU'LL NEED

- HAMMER
- NAIL PUNCH
- RAG
- WARM, SOAPY WATER
- *FOR WOOD SLIVER METHOD:*
- SLIVERS OF RECLAIMED WOOD
- WOOD GLUE
- ⚠ CHISEL AND MALLET
- *FOR PAPIER-MÂCHÉ METHOD:*
- WALLPAPER ADHESIVE (PREMIXED OR POWDERED)
- PILE OF OLD NEWSPAPERS, SHREDDED
- OLD KNIFE
- COLORED ACRYLIC CAULK, TO MATCH FLOOR OR DARKER
- CAULK GUN, IF NEEDED
- *FOR RUBBER-SEAL METHOD:*
- SCISSORS
- RUBBER SEAL, APPLICATOR
- OLD CREDIT CARD OR BLUNT KNIFE

GETTING STARTED

First, choose your method by looking at the size of the gaps, deciding whether the boards will be covered afterwards, and how beautiful you want the finish to be. The key is to allow for flexibility because floorboards move and fillers can crack.

For best results: hammer and glue in wedge-shaped slivers of reclaimed wood, then sand and treat to match the floor. Although this can be time-consuming, it is worth it, particularly if you are going to sand and treat the floorboards anyway.

Cheapest way: fill gaps with a papier-mâché of shredded newspaper and wallpaper paste, then top with a bead of acrylic caulk in a color that matches the floor. This is messy, but cost-effective, and it can be done without needing to sand the floor afterwards.

Easiest methods:

A *Branded, v-shaped plastic tape* Simply press down between boards and tape expands to fill gaps of any size. Also prevents smells from wafting up, and there's no need to treat floor afterwards. However, gaps remain and dirt can collect in the tape, which becomes hard to clean.

B *Rubber seal* Easy to install and comes in different sizes to fit range of gaps, and in dark grey color to mimic natural shadows.

For small gaps up to ¼ inch, see *Repair Scratches in Floorboards* (page 118).

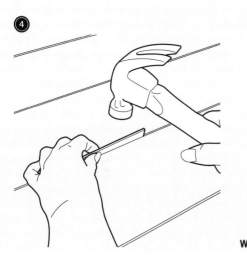

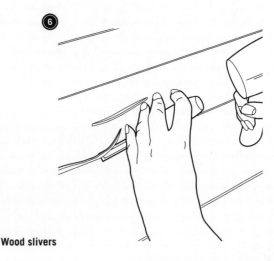

Wood slivers

WHAT TO DO

Wood slivers

1. Use a hammer and nail punch to push any protruding nails to ⅛ inch below the surface of the floorboard.

2. Clean out all floorboard gaps as thoroughly as possible and leave to dry.

3. Test out the wood slivers in the gaps for general fit. If OK, remove and apply glue down each side of sliver.

4. Place sliver into gap and hammer all over its surface to wedge it in as tightly as possible.

5. Repeat to fill all gaps in room then leave at least four hours to dry.

6. Using a chisel and mallet, carefully cut off tops of slivers to level of floor.

7. Clean away dust and dirt. Sand and varnish entire floor, as required (see pages 122-127).

Papier-mâché

1. Follow steps 1 and 2 for wood slivers.

2. If using powdered adhesive, mix up a small amount. Mix newspaper with the adhesive. Don't make it too sloppy; it needs to be able to hold up within gaps.

3. Push mixture into holes, lower than the floorboard surface. Use old knife to fill small gaps. Leave to dry thoroughly.

4. Apply acrylic caulk on top of papier mâché and leave to dry. Make sure your caulk is acrylic, not silicone – you can clean up, sand, and paint over acrylic caulk.

Rubber seal

1. Follow steps 1 and 2 for wood slivers.

2. Using scissors, push end of rubber seal into gap near baseboard. Switch to old credit card or blunt knife, and push seal in for next 2 inches.

3. Use applicator to insert remainder across floor, inserting final 2 inches with card or knife. Cut to fit at other end.

4. Push in cut end with scissors.

HOW TO NAIL IT!

- Don't use wood filler to plug gaps; manufacturers exclude floorboard filling as a use. The main reason is that it isn't flexible enough to cope with the board movements and will fall between the gaps, leaving you back where you started.

- If using wood slivers for filling gaps, try to use old or reclaimed wood. New wood can shrink over time and your gap will open up again.

- Don't use caulk by itself in floorboard gaps; it needs to rest on the papier-mâché in order to be held in place.

SAND FLOORBOARDS

Whether you are revealing your floorboards for the first time, or just refinishing them, this is a rewarding but very, very dusty job. Make sure you wear goggles and a respirator mask.

YOU'LL NEED

MATERIALS FOR PREPARING FLOOR SURFACE (SEE *GETTING STARTED*)

MASKING TAPE

DUST SHEETS, IF NEEDED

SANDER AND EDGER

COARSE-, MEDIUM-, AND FINE-GRADE SANDPAPER DISCS, AS NEEDED

SAFETY GOGGLES AND RESPIRATOR MASK

SANDPAPER SHEETS AND SANDING BLOCK, OR CHISEL

VACUUM CLEANER

SOFT CLOTH

⚠ **MINERAL SPIRITS**

MATERIALS FOR FINISHING FLOOR, AS NEEDED

GETTING STARTED

Replace and countersink any old or loose nails. See *Back to Basics* (page 18). Fill any gaps in the floorboards and repair or replace broken floorboards (see pages 119-121). The floor surface must be flat and without obstructions.

Empty the room of all furniture, pictures, and curtains. Close and seal internal doors and cupboards with masking tape. It's best if the room is completely empty, but cover anything left with dust sheets. Open windows and external doors for ventilation.

Rent the right sander for your room size and get an edger to complete the job. Read safety instructions before starting.

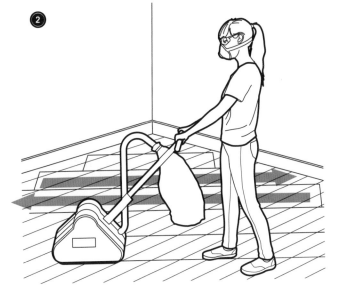

WHAT TO DO

1 Fit sander with coarse-grade sandpaper discs (or if floorboards are in good condition and not stained, you can go straight to medium-grade sandpaper). Put on goggles and respirator mask.

2 Work diagonally across the room, moving constantly and slowly, in overlapping strips.

3 If floor is deeply stained, work a second time across the room in the opposing diagonal direction.

4 Switch to medium-grade sandpaper and work up and down the room in the same direction as the boards.

5 Repeat step 4 with fine-grade sandpaper.

6 Use the edger to sand around edges of room, working through grades of sandpaper, as before.

7 Sand awkward corners with sandpaper wrapped around block, or use a chisel to scrape away dirt.

8 Wearing clean socks to avoid marking bare, untreated floor, remove all tools from the room and vacuum floor. Remove fine dust using a soft cloth dampened with mineral spirits.

9 Your freshly sanded floor will need some sort of protection or else it will stain and absorb anything spilled on it. See pages 124-127 for guidance on oiling, staining, and varnishing floorboards. For advice on painting floors, see page 156.

HOW TO NAIL IT!

- Buy more sanding discs than you think you will need. Most tool-rental companies will buy back unused discs; check with yours first.

- Check the sander dust-collection bags regularly and empty when full to prevent them from bursting. Small amounts of dust from the bags can be used to fill small holes in floorboards (see page 118).

- See *Back to Basics* (page 23) for more tips on sandpaper and sanding.

OIL FLOORBOARDS

56

Oils and waxes penetrate into the wood fibers and protect from within. Most oils and waxes are nontoxic, hypoallergenic, and easy to do minor repairs with. You'll need to reapply every one to two years. They are not as shiny or durable as other finishes. Apply oil only to freshly sanded floor. See *Sand Floorboards* (page 122).

▶ YOU'LL NEED

- STEEL TAPE MEASURE
- WOOD OIL, SUITABLE FOR FLOORS, TO COVER AREA, PLUS EXTRA
- BROOM, MOP, AND FLOOR CLEANER
- RUBBER GLOVES
- WIDE FLOOR BRUSH
- SMALL PAINTBRUSH, FOR EDGES
- LINT-FREE CLOTHS
- RAGS OR OLD CLOTHS
- **TOOL UP** POWER SANDER
- **TOOL DOWN** FINE-GRADE WIRE WOOL OR SANDPAPER AND BLOCK

⚠ STAY SAFE!

Oil-saturated cloths can spontaneously combust as the oil cures. Place in water after use, then dispose of carefully in a sealed metal container filled with water.

GETTING STARTED

Measure the room to calculate the area to be oiled. Check the oil can for guidance on coverage and remember to buy extra if you are applying more than one coat.

Make sure the room is well ventilated. Remove all furniture.

Always read and follow manufacturer's guidelines. Wear old clothes. Floorboards should be clean and dust-free.

①

WHAT TO DO

① Wearing rubber gloves, apply the oil, starting from the corner of the room farthest from the door. Apply an even layer of oil all over the floor, using a wide floor brush or paintbrush. Use a small paintbrush for edges.

② Let the wood absorb the oil for 20 minutes.

③ Add more oil if the floor is very absorbent and wait another 20 minutes.

④ Buff the oil into the wood using lint-free cloths.

⑤ Use rags or old cloths to wipe all remaining oil from the wood.

⑥ You may need two or three additional applications, depending on the manufacturer's guidelines. Before applying more coats, remove any nibs or dust. You can do this very lightly with a power sander, or with very fine-grade wire wool or sandpaper. Wipe over with damp cloth and allow to dry thoroughly.

⑦ Do not walk on floor for 12 hours after final application.

HOW TO NAIL IT!

- UV oil is a good choice if you are looking for more durability. It imparts a warm, natural look and has the durability of a lacquer.

- To keep your floor looking at its best, make your own floor polish by mixing equal parts olive oil and white vinegar. Add drops of lavender, orange, or lemon essential oil and use spray bottle to apply.

STAIN FLOORBOARDS

57

Stains and dyes color your wood, but offer no protection. They can be applied under either oil or varnish/lacquer. This job is best done by two people in one continuous process without a break. Apply stain only to a freshly sanded floor. See *Sand Floorboards* (page 122).

YOU'LL NEED

STEEL TAPE MEASURE

STAIN, TO COVER AREA, PLUS EXTRA

BROOM, MOP, AND FLOOR CLEANER

FINE-GRADE SANDPAPER

LARGE TRASH BAG

ROLLER TRAY

RUBBER GLOVES

STAINING PAD

SMALL PAINTBRUSH, FOR EDGES

LINT-FREE CLOTHS

GETTING STARTED

Measure the room to calculate the area to be stained. Check the can for guidance on coverage and remember to buy extra if you are applying more than one coat. Make sure room is well ventilated. Remove all furniture.

Always read and follow manufacturer's guidelines. Wear old clothes. Floorboards should be clean and dust-free.

All stain colors are affected by the individual color of your sanded boards, so patch-test as many inconspicuous areas as possible, then sand back again once you have made your choice.

WHAT TO DO

1 Spread out trash bag, put roller tray on it, and pour in the stain.

2 Wearing gloves, start at corner farthest from the door and apply stain with staining pad, working across two or three boards at a time. Use small paintbrush for edges. Apply quite liberally and work at a brisk pace, following line of boards. Try to cover entire boards, and do not overlap onto neighboring ones. One person should apply the stain, while the other should follow behind one minute later, wiping off any excess with a cloth and working along the grain.

3 Allow at least six hours to dry before varnishing or oiling—overnight, if possible.

HOW TO NAIL IT!

- If you have to work alone, apply stain with staining pad across a small area, then go back to the beginning and wipe off before moving on to the next boards.

- Painting your floorboards is a cost-effective way of adding color and getting a great look when your floorboards aren't so great! See *Paint Floors* (page 156).

- You can buy stains that are combined with oil, if you want color as well as the natural look of oil.

VARNISH FLOORBOARDS

Varnishes or lacquers are usually either solvent-based (highly toxic) or water-soluble (less toxic and easier to use at home). They form a durable, protective layer on top of the wood and are water-resistant. Varnishes come in various gloss levels. Apply varnish only to a freshly stained or sanded floor. See opposite and *Sand Floorboards* (page 122).

▶ YOU'LL NEED

STEEL TAPE MEASURE

VARNISH OR LACQUER TO COVER AREA, PLUS EXTRA

BROOM, MOP, AND FLOOR CLEANER

RUBBER GLOVES AND RESPIRATOR MASK

LARGE PAINTBRUSH, STAINING PAD, OR ROLLER, PLUS ROLLER TRAY

SMALL PAINTBRUSH, FOR EDGES

TOOL UP POWER SANDER

TOOL DOWN FINE-GRADE WIRE WOOL OR SANDPAPER AND BLOCK

DAMP CLOTH

GETTING STARTED

Measure the room to calculate the area to be varnished. Check can for guidance on coverage and remember to buy extra if you are applying more than one coat. Make sure room is warm and well ventilated. Remove all furniture.

Always read and follow manufacturer's guidelines. Wear old clothes. Floorboards should be clean and dust-free.

⚠ STAY SAFE!

Check manufacturer's instructions before disposing of used rags; they can be combustible.

WHAT TO DO

❶ Put on rubber gloves and respirator mask. If using staining pad or roller, pour the varnish into the roller tray.

❷ Dip pad or brush in varnish.

❸ Starting in corner farthest from door, drag pad or brush towards you along floorboard in long, smooth strokes. Use roller if covering large area. Use small paintbrush for edges. For brush, apply along grain of wood.

❹ Apply two to three coats, allowing two hours between each for varnish to dry.

❺ Before applying final coat, remove any nibs or dust. You can do this very lightly with a power sander, or with very fine-grade wire wool or sandpaper.

❻ Wipe over with damp cloth and allow to dry thoroughly, according to the manufacturer's instructions.

❼ Apply final coat and leave overnight.

HOW TO NAIL IT!

- If you are varnishing on top of a stained floor, apply at least three coats of varnish to protect the stain and give depth to the color.

- Choose combination stains-and-varnish to provide color as well as protection.

INSTALL CROWN MOLDING

59

Crown molding is the decorative molding that covers the space where the wall meets the ceiling. *Cornice* is the name for more ornate crown molding, as found in period homes. Crown molding can be made from plaster or lighter materials such as polystyrene, plastic, or wood. Most will look similar once painted; the most important thing is the shape.

YOU'LL NEED

STEEL TAPE MEASURE

CROWN MOLDING OR CORNICE MOLDING, TO COVER PERIMETER OF ROOM, PLUS EXTRA

FINE-GRADE SANDPAPER AND SANDING BLOCK

SCRAPER

DAMP SPONGE

TOOL UP COMPOUND MITER SAW

TOOL DOWN MITER BOX AND BACK SAW

WORKBENCH OR OTHER SUITABLE CUTTING SURFACE (SEE PAGE 22)

PENCIL

UTILITY KNIFE

MOLDING ADHESIVE, WITH APPLICATOR GUN

HAMMER

FINISH NAILS

PLIERS

FILLER

PAINT AND PAINTBRUSH

GETTING STARTED

Install crown molding and cornice molding before you decorate a room.

Measure the room to find the length of crown or cornice molding needed and add 20 percent for wastage.

Clean the area of loose plaster or flaking paint by sanding gently, or using a scraper. Wipe with damp sponge.

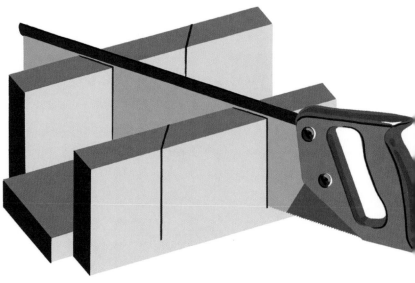

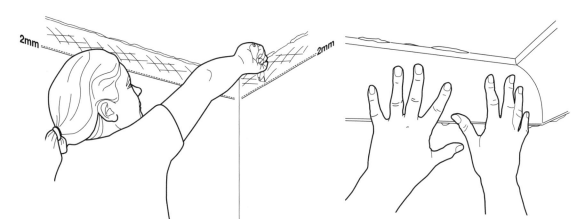

WHAT TO DO

1 Cut all lengths of crown molding using mitered cuts, following instructions for *Install Baseboards* (page 132).

2 Hold a piece of crown molding up in position and mark its dimensions on wall and ceiling in pencil, all around the room.

3 Remove any wallpaper from area to be covered by cutting it away with a sharp utility knife, staying $\frac{1}{16}$ inch within the borders of the pencil marks at each side. Pull off waste paper with a scraper.

4 If working with a plaster wall, "key" the area within guidelines by scoring the plaster with a utility knife in a crisscross pattern. This will give the adhesive grip.

5 Apply molding adhesive along both back edges of the first length of crown molding, either with applicator gun or by spreading with scraper.

6 Press molding into place within pencil guidelines, ensuring firm contact all along its length. Excess adhesive will squeeze out.

7 Remove excess adhesive with finger or scraper. Use it to fill any gaps at mitered corners or where two lengths join.

8 Using a hammer, tap finish nails into wall just below bottom edge of crown molding to support it as adhesive dries.

9 Repeat steps 2-8 until the whole area has been covered.

10 Fill any gaps with adhesive and wipe with a damp sponge. Leave adhesive to dry.

11 Lightly sand joints and corners with fine-grade sandpaper.

12 Once molding is securely in place, remove finish nails carefully with pliers, fill holes, and paint over.

HOW TO NAIL IT!

- If a wall is longer than a single length of crown molding, join two mitered lengths by butting them together with adhesive.

- Wipe away any splashes of adhesive with a damp sponge.

INSTALL CHAIR AND PICTURE RAILS

60

Chair rails divide the lower portion of the wall (the chair) from the top. Traditionally, this lower part would have been panelled. The rails can act as protection, but these days they are mainly decorative. Picture rails are usually placed 12-20 inches below ceiling height and chair rails at 36 inches from the floor.

YOU'LL NEED

STEEL TAPE MEASURE

CHAIR RAIL MOLDING, TO FIT PERIMETER OF ROOM, PLUS EXTRA

MULTIPURPOSE DETECTOR

SCREWS AND WALL ANCHORS, AS NEEDED

PENCIL

STANDARD LEVEL

LONG STRAIGHTEDGE

TOOL UP COMPOUND MITER SAW

TOOL DOWN MITER BOX AND BACK SAW

WORKBENCH OR OTHER SUITABLE CUTTING SURFACE (SEE PAGE 22)

FINE-GRADE SANDPAPER

⚠ POWER DRILL, WITH COUNTERSINK BIT, WOOD BIT AND BIT SUITABLE FOR WALL TYPE

SCREWDRIVER

SCRATCH AWL OR NAIL

WOOD FILLER

PUTTY KNIFE (OR USE FINGER)

PAINTBRUSH

PRIMER

PAINT OR VARNISH

GETTING STARTED

Measure the room to find the length of molding needed and add 20 percent for wastage.

Use a multipurpose detector to note positions of hidden pipes and cables and avoid attaching the molding there. If not attching to masonry walls, locate studs using a detector and attach to these, if possible.

See *Back to Basics* (pages 18-23) for advice on choosing screws, wall anchors, and drill bits to fit your wall, and for tips on sawing and drilling.

WHAT TO DO

1 Choose the height of your rail molding. Bear in mind how the rail will interact with other features, such as fireplaces and doorways. Mark the chosen position in pencil at each corner of the room, measuring carefully up from floor or down from the ceiling.

2 Use a standard level to get straightedge horizontal at your mark height and draw along it with pencil. Repeat across all walls.

3 Cut molding for longest wall first. Use miter saw or miter box to cut miter end, paying attention to which way angle needs to go. See *Install Baseboards* (page 132). Sand any rough edges.

4 If a wall is longer than a single length of molding, join two lengths with opposite miter cuts. Ensure both lengths are at least 12 inches long.

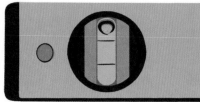

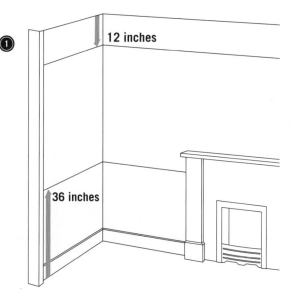

1 12 inches

36 inches

4

5 Drill small pilot holes through the molding, one 12 inches from each end and no more than a yard apart.

6 Countersink holes to ensure screw heads will be flush with surface (see page 18).

7 Hold the molding in position against the wall and mark through holes with scratch awl or nail.

8 Use appropriate bit to drill holes at marked points to depth of wall anchor, if using. If attaching to studs, drill pilot holes. Push in wall anchor, if using. Screw molding into place.

9 Repeat steps 3-7 for all the walls, making sure you cut the angle the correct way each time.

10 Cover each screw hole in the molding with wood filler. Level with putty knife or finger.

11 When dry, sand off any excess filler. Prime and paint or varnish as required. See *Paint Interior Woodwork* (page 168).

HOW TO NAIL IT!

- **If you are confused about which way a miter cut should go, remember that the back of the molding is always the same length as the wall.**

- **Don't rush the job. Measure twice and cut once.**

INSTALL BASEBOARDS

Gaps are needed between the floor and walls to allow for expansion and contraction with the weather. Baseboards hide these gaps. It's easier to prime baseboards before they go on the wall. Better still, buy primed baseboards.

YOU'LL NEED

SCRAPER

PRY BAR OR CROWBAR

STEEL TAPE MEASURE

BASEBOARD MOLDING, TO FIT PERIMETER OF SPACE, PLUS EXTRA

MULTIPURPOSE DETECTOR

NAILS AND SCREWS, SUITABLE FOR WALL TYPE

PENCIL

⬆ **TOOL UP** COMPOUND MITER SAW

⬇ **TOOL DOWN** MITER BOX AND BACK SAW

WORKBENCH OR OTHER SUITABLE CUTTING SURFACE (SEE PAGE 22)

FINE-GRADE SANDPAPER

PLUS, AS NEEDED:

FINISH NAILS AND COPING SAW

⚠ **POWER DRILL, WITH COUNTERSINK BIT, WOOD BIT, AND BIT SUITABLE FOR WALL TYPE**

SCRATCH AWL OR NAIL

SCREWDRIVER

GRAB ADHESIVE

⚠ **HAMMER**

WOOD OFFCUTS OR HEAVY BOOKS

WOOD FILLER

PAINTER'S CAULK AND CAULK GUN

PAINTBRUSH AND PAINT/VARNISH

GETTING STARTED

To remove old baseboards, gently tap a scraper down the back of the top of the boards to break the bond with the paint or any filler. Insert pry bar or crowbar and prize carefully along length of baseboards.

Measure the room to find the length of baseboard needed and add extra for wastage.

Use a multipurpose detector to find positions of hidden pipes and cables in walls and avoid attaching there.

Baseboard can be attached to the wall using nails, screws, or adhesive. Adhesive is quick, but it can be difficult to press the board close to the wall, so you may end up with gaps to fill.

Nails work well if there is something wooden to attach them to, such as a stud. Don't use nails on plasterwork.

Masonry walls: use screws and wall anchors.

Stud walls: use standard oval wire nails to attach to the studs. Use a detector to find and mark studs low down on wall.

Timber blocks: if your baseboard was originally fixed to timber blocks (a traditional way of fixing baseboards), reuse these fixing points with lost-head nails, which are stronger than oval wire nails.

Waterproof membrane: to avoid penetrating any waterproofing membrane with nails, you'll need to glue the baseboard with wood glue.

See *Back to Basics* (pages 18–23) for more advice on choosing screws, wall anchors, and drill bits to fit your wall, and for tips on sawing and drilling.

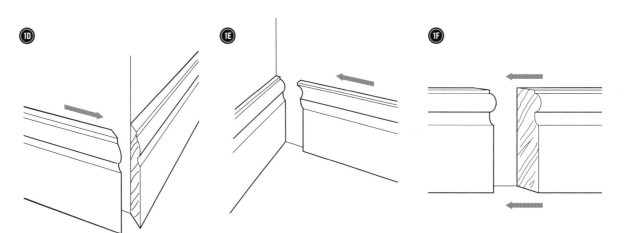

WHAT TO DO

① Cut baseboard

A Measure length of longest wall and mark position for cut in pencil on face of board. Leave shortest walls until last.

B If wall needs more than one length of baseboard, place baseboard into miter saw or box and cut at a 45-degree angle. Cut other board with opposite miter to fit. Sand any rough edges.

C Before cutting for corners, sketch out a plan for how miters will fit together.

D *External corners:* cut joining ends as a 45-degree angle, so that longest side of board is away from wall. Check that the pieces fit together before attaching.

E *Internal corners:* fit one board with flat edge into corner and secure with finish nail, tapping it in lightly. Hold second board butted at right angles to first and mark its outline on end of first board. Remove first board and cut along pencil mark with a coping saw. Refit the boards with second uncut board pushed into corner and the first board overlapping it. If you don't have a coping saw, cut boards with 45-degree miters, so that the longest part of board is against the wall.

F *At door or casing:* cut as a flat edge.

② Fix baseboard

Secure baseboard by appropriate method at existing positions, or space 2 feet apart halfway up flat part of board.

A If using screws, drill small pilot holes through board where you want them positioned, adding more if the baseboard needs pulling in due to an uneven wall. Countersink to ensure screw head will be flush with surface (see page 18).

Hold baseboard to wall and mark through the holes with a scratch awl or nail.

Use appropriate bit to drill holes at marked points to depth of wall anchor. If attaching to studs, drill pilot holes. Push in wall anchors, if using, and screw board into place.

B If using nails, mark positions of studs on baseboards. Secure with adhesive, then nail in place. Ensure nails are long enough to penetrate at least ¾ inch into studs or blocks behind. If using adhesive only, apply to back of board. Press and hold in position with wood offcuts or heavy books as props until set.

③ To finish

A Sand corners pointing into the room and fill any gaps at joins and nail holes with wood filler.

B Line the gap between baseboards and wall with caulk (see *How to Nail It!*, below). Leave to dry.

C Paint or varnish, as required.

- Install baseboards before installing new carpet (see page 106). If you're laying tiles or wooden flooring, install the baseboards last.

- Latex, acrylic, or painter's caulk is a flexible filler for imperfect joints or gaps between walls and baseboards, casings, and window frames. Unlike silicone, it can be smoothed with a wet finger or damp sponge and easily wiped away if you go wrong.

- For miter cuts, remember that the back of the baseboard is always the same length as the wall.

INSTALL WAINSCOTING

62

You can add character and texture to a room with wainscoting. It's easy to install and can be painted to great effect. This type of interior timber paneling is generally used to cover the bottom third of walls, but it can just as easily cover the whole height or even the ceiling.

▶ YOU'LL NEED

STEEL TAPE MEASURE

MULTIPURPOSE DETECTOR

PENCIL

STANDARD LEVEL

⚠ POWER DRILL WITH COUNTERSINK BIT, WOOD BIT, AND BIT SUITABLE FOR WALL TYPE

2 X ½-INCH BATTEN

SCRATCH AWL OR NAIL

WALL ANCHORS, IF NEEDED

2-INCH SCREWS AND LONGER SCREWS FOR SOCKETS

SCREWDRIVER

WAINSCOTING TO COVER SPACE, PLUS EXTRA FOR WASTAGE

TOOL UP JIGSAW OR CIRCULAR SAW

TOOL DOWN BACK SAW OR SMALL HANDSAW

WORKBENCH OR SUITABLE CUTTING SURFACE (SEE PAGE 22)

FINE-GRADE SANDPAPER

HAMMER

FINISH NAILS AND NAIL PUNCH

WOOD TRIM OR MOLDING, TO COVER TOP EDGE

WOOD GLUE

GETTING STARTED

Measure the full width of every wall you want your wainscoting to cover. It's better to space your paneling slightly so that it fits without having to cut individual pieces into thin slivers.

Double the width measurement to calculate how much batten you will need. The batten is the horizontal support that sits behind the paneling at the top and bottom.

Use a multipurpose detector to note positions of pipes and cables and avoid attaching the wainscoting there. If not attaching to masonry, locate studs using a detector and attach to these.

See *Back to Basics* (pages 18–23) for advice on choosing screws, wall anchors, and drill bits to match your wall, and for tips on sawing and drilling.

⚠ STAY SAFE!

If you're unsure about working with electricity, consult a professional electrician before attempting step 11.

⑤

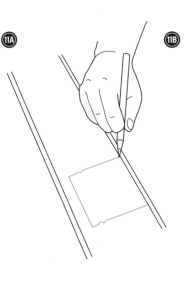

⑪A **⑪B**

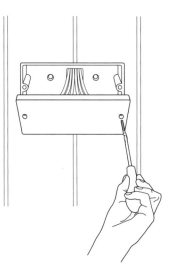

WHAT TO DO

❶ Measure and draw chosen top line on the wall with pencil, using a standard level to keep line straight. For the lower batten, mark the position as far down as possible, or just above baseboards.

❷ Drill small pilot holes all the way through batten, at intervals along its length. Countersink to ensure screws lie flush with surface. See *Back to Basics* (page 18).

❸ Hold batten to align top edge with top pencil line and mark attachment points through pilot holes onto wall with scratch awl or nail.

❹ Use appropriate bit to drill holes at attachment points to depth of wall anchor. If attaching to studs, drill pilot holes.

❺ Push in wall anchors, if using. Screw in battens so that screws are flush with surface. Repeat for lower batten.

❻ Saw wainscoting panels to appropriate length. Sand off any rough edges.

❼ Starting at one end of room, hammer in first panel with two finish nails at top and bottom, securing it to the batten behind. Use a standard level to check that the panels are straight. Recess nails just beyond wood using nail punch.

❽ Slide next panel into position and nail as before. Don't push panel in too tight; you should leave a millimeter or so to prevent buckling.

❾ Continue along length of wall. If you have to cut a panel at the end, use a jigsaw or circular saw and workbench. If you have not attempted this before, get it cut professionally.

❿ Start next wall by beginning at farthest point and working backwards, butting corners together.

⑪ A Cut around electrical outlets. Before attaching the panel, turn off the power. Mark position of outlet on relevant panel(s) and cut a smaller hole with back saw or jigsaw.

B Attach the panel(s), then secure the outlet's faceplate back on with longer mounting screws so that it sits on top of the wainscoting panel.

⑫ For a neat finish, attach trim or molding to top of panels using finish nails and wood glue. Install the baseboard around the bottom. See *Install Baseboards* (page 132).

HOW TO NAIL IT!

- If your wall is smooth, flat, and dry and if you don't think you'll be pulling off the wainscoting any time soon, then the panels can be glued directly onto the wall with grab adhesive without the use of battens. Use finish nails to hold wainscoting in place while the glue sets.

- Fill nail-punch holes with wood filler before painting.

- As long as you attach a batten measuring the same depth at the top, you can use an existing baseboard as a lower batten.

HANG PICTURES AND MIRRORS

63

One way of hanging pictures is from a picture rail (see page 130). However, if you would rather hang the pictures and mirrors individually, there are certain steps you can take to avoid marking your walls with evidence of failed attempts.

YOU'LL NEED

- MULTIPURPOSE DETECTOR
- PENCIL
- SCRAP PAPER
- MASKING TAPE
- SCRATCH AWL OR NAIL
- ⚠ POWER DRILL, WITH BITS SUITABLE FOR WALL TYPE, OR HAMMER
- HANGING DEVICE (NAIL, SCREWS, AND WALL ANCHORS, PICTURE HOOKS OR VELCRO STRIPS)
- SCREWDRIVER
- STEEL TAPE MEASURE

GETTING STARTED

It's useful to create a dummy out of paper if your picture or mirror is heavy, or if you find it hard to visualize the best position for it. Otherwise, measure carefully before drilling any holes.

See *Back to Basics* (pages 18–20) for advice on choosing screws, nails, wall anchors, and drill bits to fit your wall, and for tips on drilling.

The most secure practice is to drill into studs or attach to masonry with wall anchors. Locate studs using a multipurpose detector. Most houses have studs made of 2 x 4s, which are positioned 16–24 inches apart. Mark positions at top or bottom of wall in pencil and leave the marks on for future reference. For light loads use hollow-wall anchors away from studs on plasterboard.

Use a detector to note positions of hidden pipes and cables and avoid attaching there.

WHAT TO DO

❶ Picture or mirror with static hanger

A Set the picture or mirror on floor and place scrap paper (thicker than newspaper, preferably) over the top, taping sheets together, if necessary, to create a dummy of the same dimensions. Transfer the hanging point to the paper, too. Use this as an easier-to-handle guide for marking the hanging point on the wall.

B Hold the dummy against the wall to try out different positions, taking note of studs, if needed, and marking them on the paper. Tape the dummy in place.

C Use scratch awl or nail to punch through dummy and mark wall. Remove paper, then either tap in nail with hammer, or drill hole using appropriate bit to depth of wall anchor, or to depth of screw, if fixing to studs. Insert wall anchor, if using, and screw in your chosen hanging device.

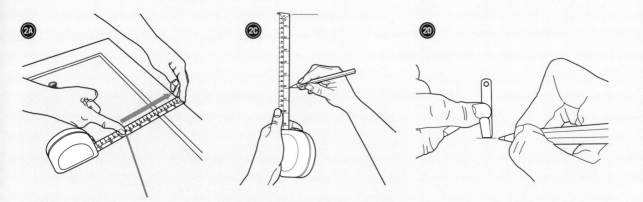

② Picture or mirror hung with wire

A Pull wire taut towards top of picture or mirror. Measure from the highest point of wire to the top of picture or mirror.

B Position on wall. Mark top of picture or mirror with pencil.

C On the wall, measure down from here the distance of the hanging wire you just noted and mark it on wall with pencil.

D Position bottom of hanging device against the lower mark and mark the hanging point. Drill hole at marked point to depth of wall anchor. If fixing to stud, drill pilot holes.

E Insert wall anchor, if using, and screw in hanging device.

③ Light picture or unframed canvas

Simply tap a picture hook or small nail into your chosen position so that ⅜ inch sticks out, angled upwards.

④ Using Velcro picture strips

These strips allow you to hang pictures and frames without the use of nails, drills, or screws. They lock together, holding the picture firmly to the wall, and are easy to remove, leaving no marks, damage, or nail holes.

Placing pictures and mirrors

Take time to consider where to hang your picture or mirror; it's great to be creative, but there are a few things to bear in mind when choosing a position.

- If you place a picture so that you have to look up at or down to it, you'll distort its perspective.

- Generally, pictures look better when they are proportionate to the size of wall: i.e. a large picture looks better on a large wall, a small picture on a small wall. If a picture is too small for your wall, add two or more pictures either side of it to create a group.

- If the pictures are too high, they will have little connection to the furniture beneath them. As a general rule, hang 6–12 inches above the back of the sofa.

- When hanging in an empty space, hang pictures so that their midpoint is somewhere around 5 feet above the floor.

- Treat groups of pictures as one picture. On the floor, arrange how you want them to fit together. Decide on your focal point, hang this at the optimum position, then fit the others around it.

- Mirrors are a great addition to any wall and not just for vanity. If hung cleverly, they can add a window to a room. They increase light and help a room look bigger.

- Ensure that mirrors are hung high enough so that your head is not cut off when you check your reflection.

HOW TO NAIL IT!

- Never drill without checking for pipes and cables.

- Ensure that you use the right screws for your walls and the weight of your picture or mirror, or it may come crashing down when you least expect it.

WALL-MOUNT TV

Flat-screen televisions are great for mounting on the wall: they are lightweight enough and can sit more or less flush. You can opt for a fixed position, a mount that will give you a small tilt, or a full-motion bracket. Stud walls or solid masonry walls are the sturdiest choice from which to hang heavy items.

▶ YOU'LL NEED

- TELEVISION MOUNT, WITH SUITABLE HARDWARE (SEE *GETTING STARTED*)
- MULTIPURPOSE DETECTOR
- PENCIL OR SCRATCH AWL
- STEEL TAPE MEASURE
- STANDARD LEVEL
- ⚠ POWER DRILL, WITH BITS SUITABLE FOR WALL TYPE
- SCREWDRIVER
- CABLE TIES AND CLAMPS, IF NEEDED

GETTING STARTED

Check that the hardware supplied is appropriate for your wall type. For masonry walls, you'll need wall anchors and screws. For cavity walls, you will need hollow wall drive anchors or toggle bolts. For stud walls, simply screw into stud. Check the wall mount to ensure that it will carry the weight of your television.

Check for hidden pipes and cables. Choose a position where the television can be seen well. If you hang it in a place you might hang a picture, you could end up with neck strain.

Flat-screen TVs are best watched head-on, so they should be at seated eye-level. Make sure direct sunlight doesn't affect the screen or it will be hard to see.

See *Back to Basics* (pages 18–20) for advice on choosing screws, wall anchors, and drill bits and for tips on drilling.

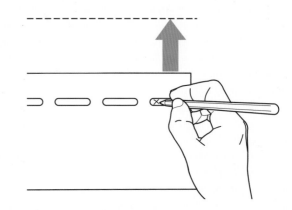

WHAT TO DO

1 Attach brackets to the back of the TV according to manufacturer's instructions. Remove plugs on the back of TV set to reveal screw holes, if necessary. Ensure that both pieces of bracket are attached in same place so that they line up evenly. Don't rest your TV face-down on the floor; it's not good for the set.

2 If not fixing to a masonry wall, find and mark studs using a multipurpose detector. In most houses, studs are made of 2 x 4s, which are positioned 16–24 inches apart. Mark central point of each stud. See *Back to Basics* (page 21) for more tips on finding studs.

3 To mark the correct position for wall mount, measure the height of the television. Loosely attach the wall part of the bracket to the TV and measure from top of wall bracket to the top of the TV. Use measurements to find the best height for the television and mark this on wall.

4 Hold bracket against wall, line up the attachment points with the studs, if using, and mark locations of holes on wall with pencil or scratch awl.

5 Use standard level to check that the marks are level. Use appropriate bit to drill holes at fixing points to depth of wall anchor, if using. If fixing to studs, drill pilot holes. Push in wall anchors, if using.

6 Secure wall mount to wall with supplied fixings. Check bracket is still level before tightening screws.

7 To hang the television on the wall: plug cables into the TV, unless the bracket allows enough space to reach the sockets, in which case do this afterwards. With a helper, lift television up onto wall bracket.

8 Check once more that the set is level.

HOW TO NAIL IT!

- A tilting wall bracket is helpful, since it allows you some access to the back of the set while installing.

- If you want a really neat finish, use a qualified electrician to provide a power source to be hidden behind the television. You can also neaten cables with cable ties and use cable clamps around baseboards.

- You may need to buy extra-long cables to account for the longer distance from the TV to the power source.

PAINTING
AND
DECORATING

EVERYTHING
YOU NEED
TO GET THE
JOB DONE

SAND WALLS

65

Careful preparation is essential if you want a professional paint finish on interior plaster walls. The first step is to sand walls down. If they have been professionally skim-plastered, you won't need to do this, but if not, sanding will give you the best starting point.

▶ YOU'LL NEED

MATERIALS FOR PREPARING WALLS (SEE *GETTING STARTED*)

DROP CLOTHS

RESPIRATOR MASK AND SAFETY GOGGLES OR GLASSES

COARSE-, MEDIUM-, AND FINE-GRADE SANDPAPER

⚡ TOOL UP POWER SANDER

↓ TOOL DOWN SANDING BLOCK

DAMP CLOTH

VACUUM CLEANER

GETTING STARTED

To remove any wallpaper, see *Strip Wallpaper* (page 160).

WHAT TO DO

1 Locate any dents, nail holes, or small cracks and fill them (anything larger may require a professional plasterer to apply skim layer). See *Fill Cracks in Plaster* (page 145) and *Fill Holes in Plaster* (page 146).

2 Lay down drop cloths to protect floors and furniture. Make sure area is well ventilated. Wearing respirator mask and safety goggles, sand the wall with coarse-grade sandpaper, using a power sander or sanding block. Wipe with damp cloth to remove dust.

3 Repeat with medium-grade sandpaper, then fine-grade sandpaper, wiping away dust with damp cloth after each sanding.

4 Repeat filling and sanding steps until wall is as smooth as you require. Vacuum away dust.

HOW TO NAIL IT!

- Choose the most expensive sandpaper you can afford; the quality does make a difference.

- You can do this job by hand or with a small power sander. For larger areas, a power sander will save you a lot of time and effort.

- See *Back to Basics* (page 23) for more tips on sandpaper and sanding.

COVER STAINS

Covering an unsightly damp patch or stain on the wall or ceiling is easy to do, as long as the original cause of the stain has been dealt with.

YOU'LL NEED

MATERIALS FOR PREPARING SURFACE (SEE *GETTING STARTED*)

DAMP CLOTH

DROP CLOTHS

STEPLADDER, IF NEEDED

STAIN-BLOCK, EITHER PAINTABLE OR SPRAY-ON

PAINTBRUSH, IF NEEDED

SAFETY GOGGLES, IF NEEDED

GETTING STARTED

Before you begin, repair any holes, cracks, or surface imperfections. See *Fill Cracks in Plaster* (opposite) and *Fill Holes in Plaster* (page 146). Sand down any rough areas. Make sure the surface of your stain is clean and dust-free by wiping down with damp cloth.

WHAT TO DO

1 Cover nearby furniture and carpets with drop cloths.

2 Open all windows and doors to help ventilate the room.

3 If the stain is on ceiling or high up the wall, put stepladder carefully in position on a level surface. Spray or brush stain-block over the stain. Work it in well, covering affected area and beyond.

4 Leave for 24 hours before painting or wallpapering.

HOW TO NAIL IT!

- There are a number of good products on the market for covering stains. Ask your local hardware store for recommendations.

- Keep the area as well ventilated as possible for as long as you can. Wear safety goggles if you are spraying stain-block above your head.

- If you have a damp stain on top of wallpaper, you will need to cut back the affected area and treat the cause of the stain before covering it and repapering. See *Hang Wallpaper* (page 162).

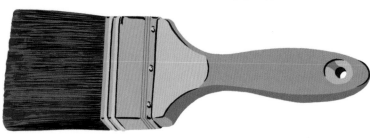

FILL CRACKS IN PLASTER

67

Plaster can crack over time purely through exposure to central heating and age. Instead of painting over the cracks, fill them properly and you shouldn't be troubled by them again. It's easier to fix big cracks than small ones, so you may need to increase the crack before you start.

YOU'LL NEED

PUTTY KNIFE OR SCRAPER

SMALL PAINTBRUSH

DAMP CLOTH

UTILITY KNIFE

VACUUM CLEANER

WATER-BASED ADHESIVE, SUCH AS WOOD OR EVEN SCHOOL GLUE (ELMER'S OR ANY PVA-TYPE GLUE), DILUTED 1 PART TO 3 PARTS WATER

LIGHTWEIGHT SPACKLING PASTE OR DRYWALL JOINT COMPOUND

FINE-GRADE SANDPAPER

PRIMER

GETTING STARTED

Carefully scrape away any loose or crumbling material with a filling knife or scraper. Use a dry paintbrush to remove any dirt or debris from around the crack. Wipe with damp cloth.

WHAT TO DO

1 Gently turn utility knife inside crack to enlarge it slightly. Remove debris and vacuum up any dust.

2 Wet the crack area, including edges, with diluted glue, or brush dipped in water.

3 Load spackling paste/compound on putty knife and draw it firmly across the crack, pressing in. Scrape excess off.

4 Leave to dry for 24 hours. Sandpaper over dried compound.

5 If the compound has shrunk at all, re-wet and fill again, repeating steps 3 and 4.

6 Paint primer over filled crack, ready for redecoration.

HOW TO NAIL IT!

- It's important to use primer before you redecorate the repaired area, or you'll always be able to see where the patch in the plaster was.

- Repaint the area using the same method (brush or roller) with which the wall was originally painted.

FILL HOLES IN PLASTER

If your existing plaster has some areas that are loose or need fixing, you can fill the problem areas without touching the "good" surface. For dealing with cracks in plaster, see *Fill Cracks in Plaster* (page 145).

YOU'LL NEED

⚠ **CHISEL**

SMALL PAINTBRUSH

DAMP CLOTH

WATER-BASED ADHESIVE, SUCH AS WOOD OR EVEN SCHOOL GLUE (ELMER'S OR ANY PVA-TYPE GLUE), DILUTED 1 PART TO 3 PARTS WATER

POWDERED OR PREMIXED PLASTER OF PARIS

CLEAN BUCKET AND STICK (IF USING POWDERED PLASTER)

PLASTERING TROWEL

PIECE OF WOODEN BATTEN

FINE-GRADE SANDPAPER AND SANDING BLOCK

PRIMER

GETTING STARTED

Remove the loose plaster: Chip away with a chisel until you reach a firm surface. Take great care not to harm the good plaster. Don't be tempted to put an implement into the hole and lever it off; this can take good plaster with it.

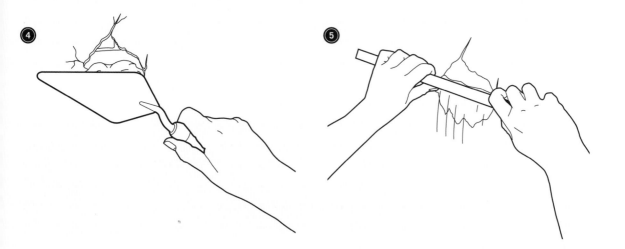

WHAT TO DO

1 Use a dry paintbrush to remove any dust. Wipe down area with damp cloth.

2 Paint over hole and edges with glue solution or water.

3 If using powdered plaster, mix in bucket using clean stick, according to manufacturer's instructions.

4 Use trowel to apply first coat of plaster to hole, pressing in firmly. Be sure to fill up to join with old plaster.

5 Use wooden batten to wipe off excess plaster, ensuring that the batten runs over new plaster and onto old plaster on all sides, so that hole will be filled to an even height.

6 Build up deep areas in layers, allowing each layer to stiffen for two hours before applying next layer. Each layer should be no more than 2 inches thick.

7 Leave to dry. Use fine-grade sandpaper lightly to sand over filled hole and surrounding area.

8 Apply primer before redecorating.

HOW TO NAIL IT!

- Some old plaster can sound hollow when tapped, but if it doesn't actually move, then it is still good and you should leave it alone. Only loose plaster should be removed.

- Don't overlook the glue stage to seal the old plaster, since it may be porous. If left unsealed, the two areas of plaster may never join properly and could develop into a new crack.

- If you don't have glue, water alone will do the trick.

PAINT CEILINGS

Paint your ceiling before painting any walls (see page 150). Your best tool is a roller with an extension handle, although it can produce paint spray, so remove anything from the room that you don't want to get speckled with paint, or cover it in a drop cloth.

▶ YOU'LL NEED

PAINT TO COVER AREA, PLUS EXTRA

STEEL TAPE MEASURE

DROP CLOTHS

TAPE AND MASKING TAPE

FEATHER DUSTER OR SOFT-BRISTLE BROOM

OLD HAT AND SAFETY GOGGLES OR GLASSES

STEPLADDER

CLEAN STICK

ROLLER TRAY

SMALL PAINTBRUSH, FOR EDGES

ROLLER, WITH EXTENSION HANDLE

GETTING STARTED

Choose the right paint for your job. See *Back to Basics* (page 24) for a guide to different paint types.

Measure the area of the ceiling. You can do this by multiplying the length by the width of the room to get a rough idea of size.

Check paint cans for guidance on coverage and remember to multiply by two if applying two coats. Round upwards in case of accidents or spills.

Empty the room and cover any furniture left with drop cloths. Protect your floors with plastic drop cloths.

Tape sheets together with regular tape, but fasten to floor edges/baseboards with masking tape.

Use a feather duster or soft-bristle broom to get rid of cobwebs and dust. Mask off any areas you don't want to get paint on.

Dress in old clothes, a hat, and goggles to keep the paint out of your hair and eyes. Open windows for ventilation.

Make sure your stepladder is positioned safely on an even surface before starting the job.

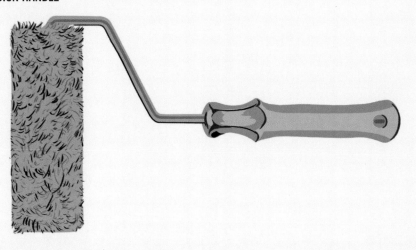

④

WHAT TO DO

1 Stir the paint with clean stick or brush and pour into roller tray reservoir, until one-third full. Take the tray up the ladder with you and rest it carefully at the top. Position yourself as safely as you can and as close to the ceiling as possible.

2 "Cut in" edges of ceiling using the small paintbrush. Paint overlapping strokes at right angles to the edge, then paint parallel to the edge in a long, sweeping motion. Place brush a fraction of an inch from edge and allow bristles to splay out as you go. See also *Paint Walls*, step 2 (page 151).

3 Move ladder to side of room and attach extension handle to roller. Dip roller into reservoir—don't overload it—and roll it up and down the tray a few times to get an even spread.

4 Paint the ceiling with roller at an angle of around 45 degrees, using light, even strokes in random directions.

5 Start each reloaded roller in an unpainted area and work back towards the last painted area.

6 Once dry, apply second coat, if desired.

HOW TO NAIL IT!

- Experiment until you get the right amount of paint on the roller; too much will send splatters everywhere, but too little will make the job go slowly. You need to think about your aching arms!

- When painting edges, you could also pour the paint into a small container that you can hold easily at the top of the ladder.

- For more painting tips, see *Back to Basics* (pages 24–27).

PAINT WALLS

This job can transform a room in hours but the key lies in the preparation. When doing any decorating job, protect your clothes with coveralls—or just wear old clothes.

▶ YOU'LL NEED

PAINT, TO COVER AREA, PLUS EXTRA

PRIMER, IF NEEDED

STEEL TAPE MEASURE

MATERIALS FOR PREPARING WALLS (SEE *GETTING STARTED*)

SOFT CLOTH OR SPONGE

⚠ **TRISODIUM PHOSPHATE (TSP) OR DISHWASHING LIQUID**

STICKY TAPE AND MASKING TAPE

PLASTIC DROP CLOTHS

STEPLADDER, IF NEEDED

CLEAN STICK

SMALL PAINTBRUSH, FOR EDGES

MEDIUM/LARGE PAINTBRUSH OR ROLLER AND TRAY

GETTING STARTED

Choose the correct paint for your job. See *Back to Basics* (page 24) for guide to paint types. Remember to prime any bare plaster first (see *How to Nail It!*, opposite).

Calculate the area to be painted by multiplying the height by width of each wall and adding together. Check paint cans for guidance on coverage and remember to multiply by two if applying two coats. Round upwards in case of accidents or spills.

If you will be painting the ceiling, too, paint it first since rollers can send paint spray down onto walls. See *Paint Ceilings* (page 148). If you will also be painting woodwork, paint that last. See *Paint Interior Woodwork* (page 168).

Prepare walls by filling any cracks or holes. Sand down to a smooth finish. If sanding a large wall, a power sander will save you a lot of time (see pages 143-147).

Using soft cloth or sponge, clean walls with TSP or warm water and a little dishwashing liquid. Leave to dry. Do this even if you think the walls are clean; grease from handprints can be invisible.

Protect your floors by taping plastic drop cloths to the floor. Tape sheets together with regular tape, but fasten to floor edges/baseboard with masking tape. Mask off any areas you don't want to get paint on. Open windows for ventilation.

Make sure your stepladder is positioned safely on an even surface before using.

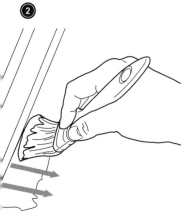

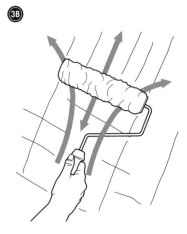

WHAT TO DO

1 Stir paint with clean stick or brush. If using a roller, pour paint into tray until one-third full.

2 To "cut in" edges: use small brush to paint overlapping strokes at right angles to the edge, then paint parallel to edge in a long, sweeping motion. Place brush a fraction of an inch from the edge and allow bristles to splay out as you go. You can paint edges before or after the main painting, but you will get a less noticeable "join" if you paint edges first.

3 Paint main wall areas in sections, starting at the window or light source and moving away in parallel bands.

A Using a brush: work in panels of around one square yard, blending each panel together while the paint is still wet.

B Using a roller: dip roller into reservoir of tray (don't overload it) and roll up and down the tray to get an even spread. With light, even pressure, hold roller at a 45-degree angle and paint in random directions. Don't go too fast. Start each reloaded roller in an unpainted area and work back towards last painted area.

4 Continue until all the walls are painted. Try to finish a complete wall before taking a break so that there's no difference in tone.

5 Leave to dry and apply second coat, as before.

HOW TO NAIL IT!

- Wrap paintbrushes and rollers in plastic wrap or a plastic bag if you take a break; there's no need to wash them. Squeeze out as much air as possible.

- To store unused paint, make sure the lid is on tightly, then turn the can upside down for a few seconds before turning it upright again for storing. This will help seal the lid with paint, so air won't penetrate and cause a skin to form on the paint.

- If painting bare plaster, dilute your first coat of paint to one part water and four parts paint and use as a seal for the porous new plaster. Follow with at least two coats of undiluted paint.

PAINT DOORS

Doors see such heavy use that they can quickly get damaged, dented, and dirty. Repairing and repainting can bring them back to life. As with all woodwork, you need to paint in the same direction as the wood grain.

YOU'LL NEED

PRIMER, IF NEEDED

SHELLAC OR RESIN-BLOCKING PRIMER-SEALER, IF NEEDED

UNDERCOAT, TO COVER AREA, PLUS EXTRA

TOPCOAT (GLOSS OR SATIN), TO COVER AREA, PLUS EXTRA

TRESTLES OR WORKBENCH, IF NEEDED

DROP CLOTHS

MASKING TAPE, IF NEEDED

DOOR WEDGE, IF NEEDED

SCREWDRIVER

MATERIALS FOR PREPARING WOOD (SEE *WHAT TO DO*)

CLEAN STICK

SMALL PAINTBRUSHES

FINE- AND MEDIUM-GRADE SANDPAPER

TOOL UP POWER SANDER

TOOL DOWN SANDING BLOCK

GETTING STARTED

Choose the right primer and paint for your woodwork. See *Back to Basics* (page 24) for guide to paint types.

Gloss, or other paint with a durable shine, will be the most hard-wearing. Never use a flat latex paint for doors; it will get dirty far too quickly. Check paint can for guidance on coverage and buy enough for two coats, if necessary.

You can paint doors in situ, or you can remove them from hinges and lay them flat on a covered floor or on trestles. See *Resize Interior Door* (page 70) for removing and rehanging a door.

Slide drop cloth under door to catch any drips.

If you're painting a glazed door, mask off the glass panels first.

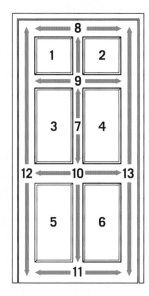

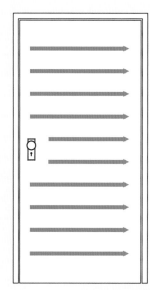

WHAT TO DO

1 If painting door in situ, use wedge to hold it open. Using a screwdriver, remove door handles. Leave wedge under door and keep a handle in your pocket, just in case you accidentally get shut inside.

2 Refer to *Paint Interior Woodwork* (page 168) for instructions on preparing and priming new wood, painted wood in good condition, and painted wood where paint is loose or crumbling.

3 Paint undercoat first, over entire primed surface.

4 Stir paint for topcoat with clean stick or brush.

5 Paint along the wood grain, holding brush perpendicular to wood. When brush begins to drag, dip it in paint to reload it. As you coat each small area, run the tips of the same "unloaded" brush over whole stretch in one long motion to smooth out the brush strokes on the paint. Smooth out the paint within one minute of it being painted on.

6 Paint hinge-side edge of door first, then outside and inside faces, as follows:

A For a paneled door: start with edges (moldings) of any panels, then panel faces, then central vertical section, followed by top, middle, and bottom crosspieces and finishing with the two side vertical sections.

B For a flush door: paint in sections from top left, working in same way as you would read a book (left to right, then down, left to right).

7 Finish by painting three exposed edges.

8 For best results, always apply a second topcoat. Sand lightly between coats.

9 When paint is dry, rehang the door, if necessary. See *Resize Interior Door* (page 70).

HOW TO NAIL IT!

- Paint both along and across the wood grain to work the paint in, but always finish a section by painting with the grain. When brush begins to drag, dip it in paint to reload it.

- When painting exterior or front doors, it's best to choose a specific front-door paint that's extremely durable, but if the color you want is not available, choose the most durable, high-gloss paint you can find.

- For more painting tips, see *Back to Basics* (pages 24–27).

PAINT STAIRWELL OR HALL

If you have mastered painting walls and ceilings, painting a stairwell or hall is only a little more difficult, mainly because some areas can be hard to reach. A roller with an extension pole is essential. Treat each area as if painting a separate room, completing one before starting the next. If you aren't using a stair ladder, you'll need an assistant to help set up scaffolding.

YOU'LL NEED

PRIMER AND PAINT FOR WALLS AND WOODWORK, TO COVER AREA, PLUS EXTRA

STEEL TAPE MEASURE

MATERIALS FOR PREPARING WALLS (SEE *GETTING STARTED*)

SOFT CLOTH OR SPONGE

⚠ TRISODIUM PHOSPHATE (TSP) OR DISHWASHING LIQUID

TAPE AND MASKING TAPE

DROP CLOTHS

FEATHER DUSTER OR SOFT-BRISTLE BROOM

TOOL UP STAIR LADDER OR SCAFFOLDING

TOOL DOWN STEPLADDER, LADDER, AND SCAFFOLD BOARDS, PLUS RAG OR OLD TOWEL

CLEAN STICK

SMALL PAINTBRUSH, FOR MOLDINGS/ CORNERS/BALUSTRADES/EDGES

ROLLER TRAY

ROLLER, WITH EXTENSION HANDLE

GETTING STARTED

Choose the right primer and paint for your walls and woodwork. See *Back to Basics* (page 24) for a guide to paint types. For high walls and ceilings, you won't have much control, so it's better to use the same color in order that mistakes won't show. Remember to prime any bare plaster first (see *How to Nail It!*, opposite). For steps, handrails, and banisters, choose a durable, high-sheen paint. These areas need to withstand a lot of traffic.

For walls, calculate the area to be painted by multiplying height by width of each wall and adding together. Check paint can for coverage and remember to multiply by two if applying two coats. Round upwards in case of accidents or spills.

Prepare walls by filling any holes or cracks. Sand down to a smooth finish. If sanding a large wall, a power sander will save you a lot of time (see pages 143–147).

Using soft cloth or sponge, clean walls with TSP or warm water and a little dishwashing liquid. Leave to dry. Do this even if you think walls are clean; grease from handprints can be invisible.

Protect floors and stairs by taping drop cloths to the floor. Tape sheets together with regular tape, but fasten to floor edges with masking tape. Be extremely careful not to create a trip hazard when working on stairs.

Protect woodwork, trims, moldings, and anything you don't want to get paint on with masking tape. Drape drop cloths over banisters.

Use duster or soft-bristle broom in high corners to get rid of cobwebs and dust. Open windows for ventilation.

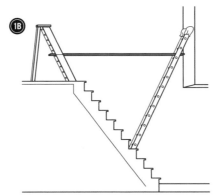

WHAT TO DO

1 Unless you are using scaffolding, or a stair ladder,

(**A**) construct a platform using a stepladder, ladder, and a scaffold board to reach both the head wall and well wall above stairway (**B**):

- Position stepladder on top landing safely back from top step.

- Wrap rag or old towel around the top of ladder so it doesn't mark walls and lean it against the head wall, with its feet resting against riser of step some way down the stairs.

- Place a scaffold board horizontally between rungs of the two ladders. Ask a friend to help and ensure you're safe.

2 Stir paint with clean stick or brush and pour into roller-tray reservoir until one-third full.

3 Paint high ceilings around stairwell opening, using small paintbrush for "cutting in" edges, and roller with extension handle for main ceiling. See also *Paint Ceilings* (page 148).

4 Cut in edges for wall area you're working on first. See *Paint Walls, step 2* (page 151). If the top of the walls is really hard to reach, try taping a brush to the extension handle.

5 Paint main wall areas in sections starting at the window or light source and moving away in parallel bands.

6 To paint wall alongside staircase: start at bottom with roller parallel to angled staircase baseboard and roll upwards in a slight curving motion until roller is traveling vertically. Paint up to middle height of wall. Use roller extension pole to work from top down and blend into wet paint on lower section.

7 To paint steps, handrails, or banisters, see *Paint Interior Woodwork* (page 168). Use a small paintbrush and remember to mask off surrounding areas.

HOW TO NAIL IT!

- If your hallways don't have much natural light, don't paint them a dark color. Choose one that complements the color of the rooms leading off the hallway. Painting walls and ceiling the same color will increase the sense of space.

- When laying protective coverings over stairs, be very careful not to make the stairs slippery. Tape down the covering along every stair so that there's no chance it will slip off. You will be looking up more than down while painting, so you won't be concentrating fully on what your feet are doing.

- If painting bare plaster, dilute first coat of flat latex to one part water and four parts paint and use as a seal for the porous new plaster. Follow with at least two coats of undiluted paint. For more painting tips, see *Back to Basics* (page 24).

PAINT FLOORS

A few thin coats wear less quickly than one thick coat, so go in sparingly with the paint. Painted wooden floorboards look great, but paint is also a good way to add interest to plywood or concrete flooring without having to install a different surface.

▶ YOU'LL NEED

PRIMER, TO SUIT FLOOR TYPE

FLOOR PAINT, TO COVER AREA, PLUS EXTRA

STEEL TAPE MEASURE

⚡ **TOOL UP** POWER SANDER

▼ **TOOL DOWN** SANDING BLOCK

MASKING TAPE

CLEAN STICK

SMALL PAINTBRUSH, FOR EDGES

LARGE NATURAL-BRISTLE BRUSH

ROLLER TRAY

ROLLER (OPTIONAL)

FINE-GRADE SANDPAPER

PAINT SEALER, IF NEEDED

FOR WOODEN FLOORBOARDS:

DROP CLOTHS

RAG OR LINT-FREE CLOTH

⚠ MINERAL SPIRITS

FOR OTHER SURFACES:

BROOM AND MOP OR SPONGE, AS NEEDED

⚠ TSP OR FLOOR CLEANER

GETTING STARTED

Choose a primer appropriate to your floor type and a specialist floor paint, which will be much more durable than a standard paint.

Calculate the area to be primed and painted by multiplying the length of room by its width. Check paint cans for guidance on coverage and don't forget to allow for at least two coats, ideally three. Round upwards.

Remove all furniture and pictures from room and open windows for ventilation.

If you will be sanding wooden floorboards, put drop cloths over any remaining items in the room, such as built-in cabinets. Wear old clothes!

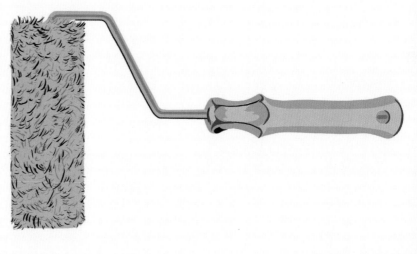

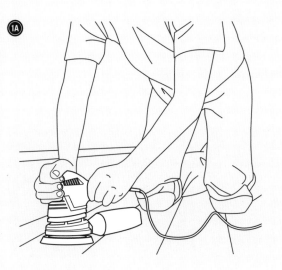

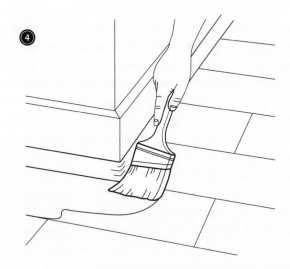

WHAT TO DO

1 A If painting wooden floorboards, you will need to sand them first. Use fine-grade sandpaper and a power sander or block to sand floor lightly. For a large area, or a floor with lots of imperfections, consider renting a larger sander. See *Sand Floorboards* (page 122). Remove fine dust using soft cloth dampened with mineral spirits.

B For other surfaces, sweep, then clean floor with TSP or floor cleaner, and mop or sponge.

2 Protect baseboards with masking tape and apply primer, depending on floor type (a concrete floor will require a different primer than a wooden floor). Leave to dry overnight.

3 Stir paint with clean stick or brush and pour into reservoir of roller tray until one-third full.

4 Cut in edges first. Use small brush to paint overlapping strokes at right angles to the edge, then paint parallel to edge in long sweeping motion. Place brush a fraction of an inch from edge and allow the bristles to splay out as you go.

5 Start at the farthest corner of the room so that you can paint your way out. Apply the first thin coat of paint with a natural-bristle brush; this creates a smooth finish. A roller will create a stippled finish. If painting floorboards, follow the grain of the wood.

6 Leave to dry for 24 hours.

7 Apply two more thin coats, allowing 24 hours before applying the next coat. Give the floor a light sand between coats.

8 Depending on the paint type, you may need to apply a paint sealer.

HOW TO NAIL IT!

- If it isn't a warm day, keep the heating on while painting to help the paint dry without wrinkling.

- After the final coat of paint, it's acceptable to walk on the surface in socks after 24 hours. Leave your floor a few days longer before dragging furniture back into place—and no high heels for a month!

- If you want a white stain on floorboards, apply a thin coat of white flat latex paint, thinned with water. Allow to dry, then apply three coats of water-based varnish. Alternatively, mix a small amount of white flat latex paint (around two teaspoons) with about a cup of water-based varnish to make a tint. After the first coat, either apply two coats of untinted varnish or another tinted layer, depending on the color you want.

PAINT RADIATOR

74

Unless your radiators are very rusty you should be able to paint them in situ. Depending on the type of radiator you have, you may want to choose a long, angled brush to help you get into awkward spaces. Spray paint can give you a really good finish.

▶ YOU'LL NEED

HIGH-HEAT RADIATOR PAINT
(CAN OR SPRAY)

MASKING TAPE

DROP CLOTH

RESPIRATOR MASK

FINE-GRADE SANDPAPER

▲ **TOOL UP** POWER SANDER

▼ **TOOL DOWN** SANDING BLOCK

SOFT CLOTH OR SPONGE

⚠ TSP OR DISHWASHING LIQUID

ANTI-CORROSIVE METAL PRIMER
OR OIL-BASED UNDERCOAT,
IF NEEDED

▲ **TOOL UP** RADIATOR PAINT ROLLER
OR LONG, ANGLED PAINTBRUSH

▼ **TOOL DOWN** PAINTBRUSH

SCRAP CARDBOARD, SAFETY
GOGGLES, AND RESPIRATOR MASK, IF
USING SPRAY PAINT

GETTING STARTED

Choose your paint. It should be heat-resistant and designed specifically for painting metal.

Turn heating off and let the radiator cool completely before you begin.

Mask off areas not being painted and lay down a drop cloth to protect floor underneath.

Radiator rollers are actually made for painting the wall behind radiators, but the long handle and small head can also be useful for reaching the visible parts at the back of the radiator. If you have a radiator with deep ridges, an angled paintbrush is a good option.

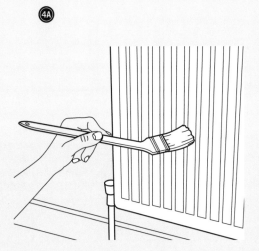

WHAT TO DO

1 Wearing mask, sand down radiator. You may find holding a piece of sandpaper easier. Make sure you sand any rusted areas really well.

2 Using soft cloth or sponge, clean radiator with TSP or warm water and a little dishwashing liquid. Rinse with warm water and cloth and dry with soft cloth.

3 Paint metal primer or an oil-based undercoat over any bare metal or previously rusted areas.

4 Apply two coats of radiator paint, leaving four hours for drying between coats. Keep the coats as thin as possible to avoid drips.

A Use a medium-to-small brush, or an angled brush to get inside ridges.

B A radiator roller is also useful for painting visible areas behind the radiator.

C To spray-paint the radiator, cover all surrounding areas with drop cloths and make sure area is well-ventilated. Wear safety goggles and a respirator mask and read manufacturer's instructions. Put cardboard between the radiator and the wall to prevent the paint from going onto the wall.

5 Make sure paint is completely dry before turning radiator back on.

HOW TO NAIL IT!

- If your radiator has thick paint with drip marks, paint stripper will do a better job than sandpaper of getting down to a workable surface. Don't forget to wear protective gloves, goggles, and a respirator mask before using stripper, and read manufacturer's instructions.

- A standard undercoat or primer won't prevent cracking or discoloration. Make sure you use the appropriate paint and primer and ask for advice if you are unsure.

- Don't paint over bolts or moving parts; you could seal them shut.

STRIP WALLPAPER

Dont be tempted to put new wallpaper on top of old, unless the finish is excellent. Not only will it make your job harder later, but the imperfections in the paper underneath can affect your beautiful new paper. When stripping wallpaper, patience is the key. Soak and wait, soak and wait, soak and wait again!

▶ YOU'LL NEED

UTILITY KNIFE

TOOL UP WALLPAPER SCORING TOOL

TOOL DOWN UTILITY KNIFE

TOOL UP STEAM STRIPPER (BUY OR RENT), PLUS PROTECTIVE GLOVES

TOOL DOWN WARM WATER, DISHWASHING LIQUID, AND SPONGE

WIDE SCRAPER

GETTING STARTED

If using a steam stripper, wear long sleeves and gloves to protect yourself.

Test ease of stripping by prizing up a corner of wallpaper with utility knife. Pull paper up with even, moderate pressure, keeping it close to the wall. If it comes away easily, continue. If it doesn't come away, follow the steps opposite.

Some walls may be easier than others, particularly in kitchens and bathrooms where the air is generally more moist. In addition, some papers are designed to be easier to peel off than others.

Be especially careful with drywall. You can easily damage the paper and gypsum layers and end up having to replaster!

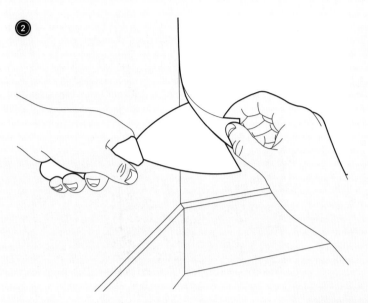

WHAT TO DO

Score wallpaper by making a series of shallow, crisscross cuts with wallpaper scoring tool or utility knife. Be careful not to score the wall underneath. The more holes there are in the paper, the wetter it can get and the softer it will be.

Strip the wallpaper using one of the following methods:

Sponge

1 Working from bottom of wall, soften scored wallpaper with soapy sponge and leave for about five minutes. Slide scraper under edge of paper to see if it's ready to strip. If not, sponge down again.

2 Try to pull away first strip. If it needs help, slide scraper under paper and push it up underneath, holding it at a 30-degree angle. If paper tears, wet it and try again.

3 Clean up glue residue by wiping down with sponge and warm, soapy water.

4 Leave to dry for at least two days before redecorating.

Steam stripper

1 Fill tank with water and switch on. Once light comes on and steam appears from the plate, it's ready to use.

2 Working across from bottom of wall, place steamer plate on top of wallpaper for about 30 seconds to one minute. Hold the plate in one hand and use the other to scrape the area you have just softened. If paper tears, wet it again with steam stripper and try again.

3 Clean up glue residue by wiping down with sponge and warm, soapy water.

4 Leave to dry for at least two days before redecorating.

HOW TO NAIL IT!

- If using water and sponge on hard-to-remove wallpaper, make your own stripping solution. Mix fabric conditioner with water at a ratio of one part conditioner to two parts water. Alternatively, mix one part vinegar to three parts water. You could also add a handful of wallpaper paste to your bucket of soapy water to help hold the water on the wall.

- Clean off the scraper regularly. As the glue builds up, the scraper has to work harder.

- You could use a spray bottle instead of a sponge as a quick way of dampening the entire area.

HANG WALLPAPER

Wallpapering is the easiest way to bring pattern to a living space and can create dramatic effects. You should hang wallpaper as the final decoration stage, after you've painted ceilings and woodwork. Remember that walls are rarely straight, so line up your paper to a plumb line (a piece of string with a weight at the end) rather than a corner.

▶ YOU'LL NEED

- STEEL TAPE MEASURE
- WALLPAPER, TO COVER AREA, PLUS EXTRA
- DROP CLOTHS
- MATERIALS FOR PREPARING WALLS (SEE *GETTING STARTED*)
- SOFT CLOTH OR SPONGE
- ⚠ TSP OR DISHWASHING LIQUID
- WALLPAPER PASTE, TO FIT YOUR WALLPAPER TYPE
- SCREWDRIVER
- STRING, THUMBTACK, AND WEIGHT
- PENCIL
- RULER OR LONG STANDARD LEVEL
- WALLPAPER SCISSORS
- MATERIALS FOR PASTING WALLPAPER (SEE PAGE 164)
- STEPLADDER
- WALLPAPER SMOOTHING TOOL OR PAPER-HANGING BRUSH
- WET SPONGE AND CLEAN RAG
- WIDE SCRAPER
- UTILITY KNIFE
- WALLPAPER SEAM ROLLER

GETTING STARTED

Measure room area to calculate how much wallpaper you'll need. Include spaces for windows and doors as you will need extra for wastage.

Move as much furniture out of the room as possible and cover anything left with drop cloths.

Prepare walls by filling any holes or cracks. Sand to a smooth finish. If working on a large area, a power sander will save you a lot of time (see pages 143-147).

Using soft cloth or sponge, clean walls with TSP or warm water and a little dishwashing liquid. Leave to dry.

If walls are bare plaster, apply a coat of diluted wallpaper paste to the entire area to prevent it from absorbing too much paste.

Turn off electricity to the room. Using screwdriver, remove light switches and outlet covers (only do this after you've washed the walls and once they are dry). See also *Wallpaper Around Obstacles* (page 166).

Choose a corner of the room to start wallpapering. Work from left to right if you are right-handed and vice-versa if you are left-handed.

Measure height of your first wall. The easiest way is to secure a piece of string at the top of wall with a thumbtack, run it taut down to the baseboard, mark the length, remove, and measure alongside tape measure. Keep the string and thumbtack to make your plumb line.

⚠ STAY SAFE!

If in any doubt about working with electricity, always consult a professional.

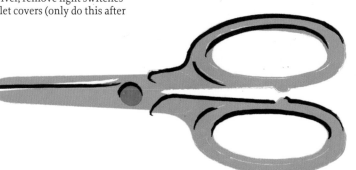

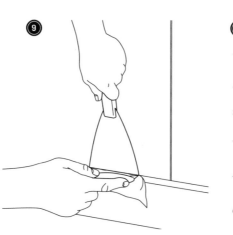

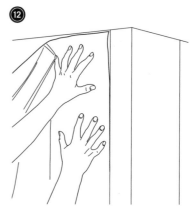

WHAT TO DO

1 If you are only papering one feature wall, start in the middle and work to sides. If you are papering an entire room, the key is to keep the paper vertical, even if corners are not.

2 To get your first vertical line, hang a plumb line (a weight attached to a piece of string) a little distance from your starting corner. Secure with a thumbtack. Mark the position of line down the wall, using plumb line as a guide. Join marks using a ruler or standard level. This will give you a perfect vertical line as a guide for your wallpaper.

3 Unroll the paper, pattern-side down, on pasting table. Measure, mark, and cut 4 inches longer than the height of wall from ceiling to baseboards so that you allow for final trimming.

4 Apply wallpaper paste (see page 164). If using pre-pasted wallpaper you can skip this step, although professionals usually paste even pre-pasted wallpaper.

5 Check which way up the pattern goes before bringing the paper to the wall. On stepladder, align first sheet with the vertical line you drew, with approximately 4 inches spare paper overhanging at baseboards. Position it to the side of the line nearest starting point so that a small amount of paper goes around the corner.

6 Use wallpaper smoothing tool or paper-hanging brush to smooth from middle outwards with medium pressure, being careful not to stretch the paper.

7 To remove wrinkles and bubbles, gently pull the edge of paper away from wall until they disappear. Smooth the paper back to wall, from middle out.

8 Clean any excess adhesive using wet sponge. Wipe dry with clean rag.

9 Trim off excess paper at bottom by pressing wide scraper where paper meets baseboard, then running a utility knife along the crease line.

10 Repeat steps 4–9 with second sheet, aligning it with first sheet and matching up any patterns. If patterned wallpaper doesn't seem to line up absolutely along whole length, prioritize matching it up at eye level.

11 Secure joints with seam roller (gently, without squeezing out the adhesive) and repeat 10–15 minutes later.

12 When you reach a corner, remember to run around it, rather than butting sheets together at corners. If you have to, overlap sheets. Before pasting the first sheet of the next wall, always line up the paper with a new plumb line to make sure corners or uneven walls don't knock it out of line on your new wall.

13 Lap the final sheet over first sheet. Clean any excess adhesive using wet sponge. Wipe dry with clean rag.

HANG WALLPAPER
APPLY PASTE

**WALLPAPER PASTE,
TO FIT YOUR WALLPAPER TYPE**

PASTE BUCKET

ROLLER TRAY (OPTIONAL)

LONG PASTING TABLE

PASTING BRUSH OR PAINT ROLLER

GETTING STARTED

Some wallpapers don't need pasting; they come pre-pasted, or are designed to be hung against a pasted wall. However, a professional decorator will usually paste even pre-pasted wallpaper.

The traditional method—and still the most common—is to apply wallpaper paste to the back of the paper. You can buy colored wallpaper paste that dries clear, to help identify any areas that may have been missed.

It's important to let the paste soak into the paper before you hang it; the paper will expand slightly with the paste, and if you hang it too soon, air bubbles may appear. Keep your work space clean between sheets, but don't worry too much about spills—the paste is water-soluble.

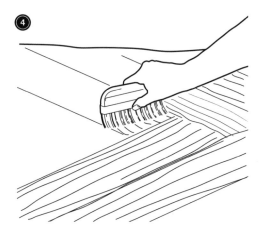

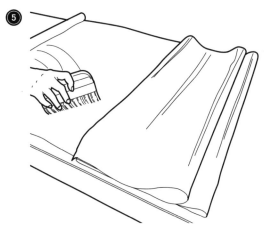

WHAT TO DO

1 Mix the paste in a paste bucket according to the manufacturer's instructions. Pour it into a roller tray, if you prefer.

2 Lay cut length of wallpaper face-down on pasting table, with one end overhanging table.

3 Load brush or roller with paste, wiping off excess by dragging it across edge of bucket or tray. Paste along center of whole length on table, leaving overhanging piece unpasted. If paper is shorter than the pasting table, weigh down one end to stop it rolling back on itself.

4 Work paste out towards edges from center in a herringbone pattern.

5 If paper is longer than table, loosely accordian-fold the pasted paper over itself—be careful not to crease it— and carefully move folds to one end, bringing up unpasted paper onto the table.

6 Repeat steps 2-4 until whole length of paper has been pasted.

7 Leave pasted folds of paper to soak up paste for as long as manufacturer recommends (usually five minutes). Hang the paper (see page 162).

8 Wipe off any spilled paste from table using clean, wet sponge.

9 Paste up more lengths and leave to soak before hanging.

HOW TO NAIL IT!

- When cutting damp wallpaper it can easily pull and tear. Ensure your blade is super-sharp.

- Don't let the roll of paper drop suddenly when you first position it at the top of the room, or its weight could tear or stretch the paper.

- Hanging lining paper first will give you a smoother surface for your wallpaper: a good way to disguise bumpy or uneven walls. Hang it horizontally or, if hanging it vertically, make sure the seams of two wallpaper layers don't fall in same place.

WALLPAPER AROUND OBSTACLES

77

The best way to wallpaper around obstacles—including radiators, heating or air-conditioning vents, wall anchors, electrical outlets, or light switches—is to remove them from the wall. This isn't always possible, so there are tricks for working around them.

▶ YOU'LL NEED

VACUUM CLEANER OR BRUSH
PENCIL
WALLPAPER SCISSORS
NARROW PAINT OR WALLPAPER ROLLER
MATCHSTICK
WIDE SCRAPER
UTILITY KNIFE
SCREWDRIVER
SMALL PAINTBRUSH

GETTING STARTED

Ensure electricity is switched off completely to the room if you are going to be papering around electrical outlets and light switches.

⚠ STAY SAFE!

If in any doubt about working with electricity, always consult a professional.

WHAT TO DO

Paper around radiator

❶ Turn off the heat and wait for radiator to cool. Clean dust and dirt behind radiator.

❷ Wallpaper up to the side of the radiator and tuck paper in behind radiator until you reach the supporting bracket. Hang the next sheet over the front of the radiator, flattening it as close to the radiator as possible. Mark position of the top point of bracket.

❸ Cut vertical line from bottom of paper up to top point of radiator bracket. Cut small rectangle at top of slit.

❹ Push paper behind radiator and into place around bracket using narrow paint or wallpaper roller.

❺ Rejoin paper underneath radiator and trim at baseboards as normal. See *Hang Wallpaper* (page 162).

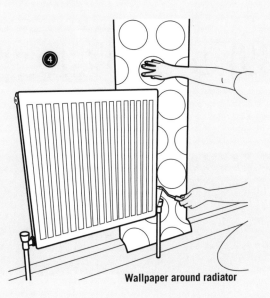

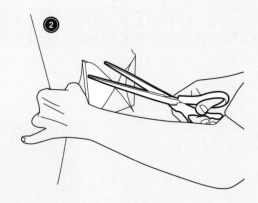

Wallpaper around radiator

Wallpaper around light sockets and switches

Paper over wall hardware

1 Remove hardware, such as picture hooks, or screws from wall anchors.

2 Stick matchstick into wall anchor so it stands slightly away from the wall. Press stick through paper as you bring it over and smooth paper around hole. Remove matchstick and replace the hardware.

Paper around door frame

1 Hang a full-length pasted strip so that one side of it overlaps the door.

2 Make a diagonal cut from the loose edge back to top corner of door frame.

3 Smooth down paper up to the door frame. Trim off any excess by pressing a wide scraper where paper meets door frame, then running a utility knife along the crease. Alternatively, pull the paper slightly away from wall and cut with scissors along the crease line.

4 Repeat on other side in reverse, butting up to first strip.

Paper around light sockets and switches

1 Hang pasted paper over the socket or switch and smooth gently so it makes impression on paper. Be careful not to tear the paper.

2 Pierce a hole at center with scissors and cut along lines to corners. Pull back flaps.

3 Trim flaps, leaving overlap of around ⅝ inch of paper on socket or switch.

4 Double-check that the electricity is turned off. Using screwdriver, partially unscrew faceplate and pull it ⅝ inch away from the wall.

5 Carefully ease paper overlap behind faceplate and use paintbrush to smooth away any air bubbles. Secure faceplate back in place.

6 Let paste dry before turning the electricity back on.

HOW TO NAIL IT!

- An alternative way to wallpaper behind a radiator is to cut the sheet horizontally, all the way across, just above the top of the radiator bracket. Then, take a separate length of paper and paste it from the base of the baseboard to meet the bottom of the radiator bracket.

PAINT INTERIOR WOODWORK

Door frames, window frames, and baseboards will be more durable and look better if they've been painted properly. Good preparation is key, so make sure you prepare your surfaces well before opening the paint cans.

YOU'LL NEED

UNDERCOAT, TO COVER AREA, PLUS EXTRA

TOPCOAT (GLOSS OR SATIN), TO COVER AREA, PLUS EXTRA

TAPE AND MASKING TAPE

PLASTIC DROP CLOTHS

FINE- AND MEDIUM-GRADE SANDPAPER

⚡ **TOOL UP** POWER SANDER

⬇ **TOOL DOWN** SANDING BLOCK

CLOTH OR SPONGE

PAINTBRUSHES

PLUS, AS NEEDED:

PRIMER

SHELLAC, OR RESIN-BLOCKING PRIMER-SEALER

SCRAPER

⚠ TSP OR DISHWASHING LIQUID

WOOD FILLER

FLEXIBLE PUTTY KNIFE

PAINTER'S CAULK AND CAULK GUN

GETTING STARTED

Choose the right primer and paint for your woodwork. See *Back to Basics* (page 24) for guide to paint types and painting tips. Remember that ordinary wall and ceiling paint will not last long on woodwork; something with a high sheen, like gloss, is the most durable. You may need to apply shellac plus primer, or resin-blocking primer-sealer, on new or bare wood.

Protect your floors by taping down plastic drop cloths. Tape sheets together with regular tape, but fasten to floor edges/baseboard with masking tape. In each case, mask off areas not to be painted.

③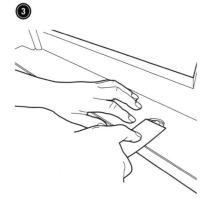

⑦

⑨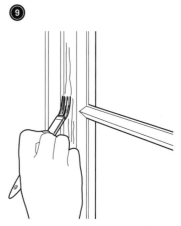

Wood where paint is loose or crumbling

WHAT TO DO

New wood

❶ Sand down area to be painted with fine-grade sandpaper, using either a power sander or sanding block. Wipe down with damp cloth.

❷ Mask off areas not to be painted and paint wood with shellac and primer, or resin-blocking primer-sealer. This stops resin seeping through and staining the surface over time.

❸ Sand lightly with fine- or medium-grade sandpaper, as above. Wipe down with damp cloth.

❹ Paint on undercoat.

❺ Finish with topcoat. Paint along the wood grain with chosen paint, holding brush perpendicular to wood. When brush begins to drag, dip it in paint to reload it. As you coat each small area, run the tips of the same "unloaded" brush over whole stretch in one long motion to smooth out the brush strokes on the paint. Do this smoothing out within one minute of the paint being applied.

❻ If the paint looks a little streaky, or if the coverage isn't good enough once dry, sand lightly again, and apply a second coat. This will also give the most durable finish.

Painted wood in good condition

If the previous paint is in good condition or you simply want to freshen things up, sand as for new wood. Wipe down with a damp cloth and paint on a new topcoat. Add a second coat if required.

Wood where paint is loose or crumbling

❶ Remove loose paint with scraper.

❷ Using cloth or sponge, clean area with TSP or warm water and a little dishwashing liquid. Wipe down with a damp cloth.

❸ Fill any cracks, holes, chips, and dips in the wood with wood filler. Apply with flexible putty knife. Refer to *Repair Rotten Window Frame* (see page 82) if you are painting a window frame and find any soft areas of wood. Scrape off excess filler and leave to dry.

❹ Sand entire area with medium-grade sandpaper, following with fine-grade, if necessary. Make sure filled areas are smooth. Wipe down with damp cloth.

❺ If you need to replace glazing compound, see *Replace Broken Windowpane* (page 84).

❻ Fill any gaps between woodwork and wall/floor, or at joints, with painter's caulk (see page 133).

❼ Paint shellac and primer, or resin-blocking primer-sealer, over any exposed knots or bare wood. Once dry, sand with fine- or medium-grade sandpaper.

❽ Follow with undercoat. For best results, use two coats, especially if you are covering a strong color.

❾ Finish with topcoat, applying it as for new wood (see step 5). If the paint looks a little streaky or if the coverage isn't good enough once dry, sand lightly again and apply second coat.

HOW TO NAIL IT!

- Don't ignore the sanding stage. This "keys" the surface so that new paint can adhere properly. If you paint straight onto gloss, the new paint will soon come away.

- To find all imperfections in wood that need filling, shine a flashlight over the area and mark your findings in pencil.

- If painting window frames, paint early in the day to maximize the time you can keep the window open for drying.

PAINT EXTERIOR WOODWORK

Exterior woodwork is likely to need thorough cleaning before you can do anything with it—nobody can paint over cobwebs. Good preparation will not only make the woodwork look better, but it's essential for protecting and prolonging its life. If your woodwork rots, it will be expensive to repair or replace.

▶ YOU'LL NEED

UNDERCOAT, TO COVER AREA, PLUS EXTRA

EXTERIOR TOPCOAT (GLOSS OR SATIN), TO COVER AREA, PLUS EXTRA

FINE-, MEDIUM-, AND COARSE-GRADE SANDPAPER

⚡ **TOOL UP** POWER SANDER

⚡ **TOOL DOWN** SANDING BLOCK

CLOTH OR SPONGE

PAINTBRUSHES

PLUS, AS NEEDED:

EXTERIOR PRIMER

SHELLAC, OR RESIN-BLOCKING PRIMER-SEALER

SCRAPER

⚠ **TSP OR DISHWASHING LIQUID**

SCRUBBING BRUSH

WOOD FILLER

FLEXIBLE PUTTY KNIFE

MASKING TAPE

GETTING STARTED

Choose a dry, still day and never paint wet wood; check the weather forecast first. See *Back to Basics* (page 24) to help you choose the right primer and paint for your woodwork. Select a weatherproof exterior wood paint; ordinary wall and ceiling paint is not suitable for woodwork, especially outdoors.

WHAT TO DO

Bare wood

Sand, prime, and paint wood following instructions for *Paint Interior Woodwork* (page 169).

Painted wood in good condition

If the previous paint is in good condition or to freshen things up, sand it lightly, wipe down with a damp cloth, and paint with two coats of exterior topcoat.

Wood where paint is loose or crumbling

❶ Remove loose paint with scraper.

❷ Using a cloth or sponge, clean area with TSP or warm water and dishwashing liquid. Use a scrubbing brush for droppings or hard deposits. Wipe with damp cloth.

❸ Fill any cracks, holes, chips, and dips as for *Paint Interior Woodwork* (page 169). Sand area using coarse-, medium-, or fine-grade sandpaper, depending on roughness of surface. Finish with fine-grade. Wipe with damp cloth.

❹ Coat any exposed bare wood with shellac and primer, or resin-blocking primer-sealer. Sand down with fine-grade sandpaper.

❺ Follow with one coat of exterior undercoat.

❻ Finish with exterior topcoat, as for *Paint Interior Woodwork* (see *New wood*, step 5, page 169). For the best finish and durability, use two coats, sanding in between once fully dry.

HOW TO NAIL IT!

- If you're painting all the exterior woodwork at your home, start at the top and work down, planning realistic amounts each day.

- Refer to *Repair Rotten Window Frame* (see page 82) if painting a window frame and find any areas of soft wood. To replace glazing compound, see *Replace Broken Windowpane* (page 84).

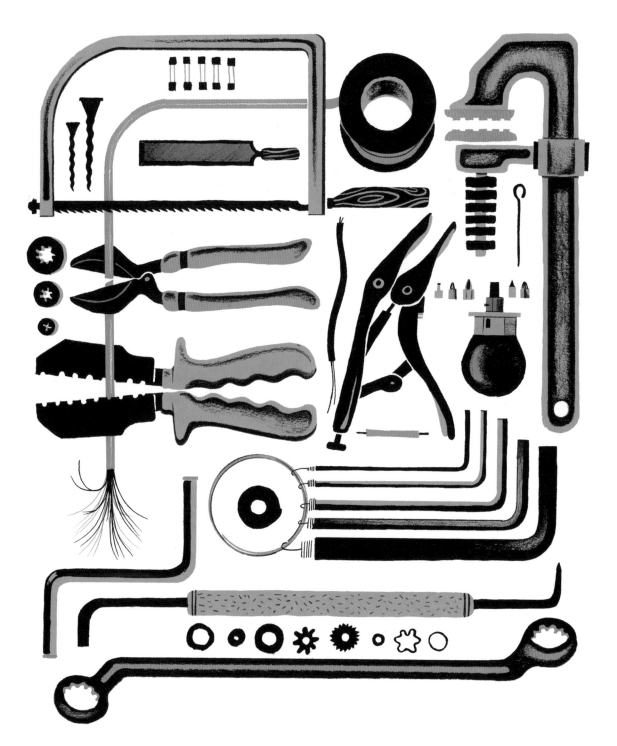

STORAGE AND FURNITURE

EVERYTHING YOU NEED TO GET THE JOB DONE

INSTALL FLOATING SHELVES

80

If you don't like being able to see shelf brackets, a more attractive option is to fit floating shelving. Thick floating shelves look great and seem strong, but they can only support light or medium weights. If you want to have stronger floating shelves, the method is more complex.

▶ YOU'LL NEED

MULTIPURPOSE DETECTOR

FLOATING SHELF SET

STANDARD LEVEL

SCRATCH AWL OR NAIL

⚠ **POWER DRILL, WITH BIT SUITABLE FOR WALL TYPE**

SCREWS AND WALL ANCHORS, AS NEEDED

SCREWS

SCREWDRIVER

GETTING STARTED

Choose a stretch of flat wall for your shelves and use a multipurpose detector to check for hidden pipes or cables. On a stud wall, use the detector to locate the studs. Use these as attachment points.

1 Hold metal strip in position on wall, using a standard level to check that it's horizontal. Mark screw holes on wall using scratch awl or nail.

2 Drill holes with suitable bit to the depth of wall anchor, if using, and push in. If fixing to studs, drill pilot holes. Screw metal strip in place.

3 Fit the shelf onto the bars and secure with screws, if provided.

HOW TO NAIL IT!

- For more help on finding and fixing to studs, see *Back to Basics* (page 21).

INSTALL SIMPLE SHELVES

The simplest way to fit shelves is with brackets. These come in a variety of styles, from basic adjustable brackets to more ornate-looking ones, with a number of different materials and finishes. Buy precut shelves and brackets to match. Some shelves may come with predrilled holes.

▶ YOU'LL NEED

SHELF/SHELVES

MULTIPURPOSE DETECTOR

PENCIL

STEEL TAPE MEASURE

2 BRACKETS PER SHELF (MORE IF REQUIRED, DEPENDING ON LENGTH)

STANDARD LEVEL

SCRATCH AWL OR NAIL

⚠ POWER DRILL, WITH SMALL TWIST BIT AND BIT SUITABLE FOR WALL TYPE

WALL ANCHORS, IF NEEDED

LONG SCREWS, TO GO 1 INCH INTO WALL

SHORTER SCREWS, FOR SHELVES

SCREWDRIVER

GETTING STARTED

Choose shelves to match your room style and the load they will hold. The different materials, listed below, vary in strength and cost.

Particle board: chips of wood glued together. The cheapest material and easy to cut to size and fix. Available with melamine or wood veneers.

MDF: medium-density fiberboard. Wood fibers stuck together under pressure. Can be painted, stained, or varnished.

Blockboard: layers of soft wood between two layers of veneer. Still cheaper than solid wood and very strong.

Plywood: thin sheets of wood glued together with the grain running in alternating directions.

Solid wood: seal your preferred wood with wax or varnish to protect it from dirt and for a natural finish.

Glass: should be at least $\frac{1}{4}$ inch thick. Requires medium- or heavyweight brackets. Use toughened glass.

Choose from fixed or adjustable brackets and make sure they match the size of the shelves and the weight they will bear. Make sure the brackets don't extend past the depth of the shelf.

Fixed: simple supports best suited to single shelves.

Adjustable: tracks fix to the wall to take a series of brackets at suitable intervals. Fully adjustable, but because the tracks and brackets are visible to the eye, less pretty to look at.

Screws should go into wall by 1 inch, at the very least, with shorter ones needed for the shelf. If screws come with the brackets make sure they are the right size and type for your wall.

See *Back to Basics* (pages 18–20) for more advice on choosing screws, wall anchors, and drill bits to fit your wall, and for tips on drilling.

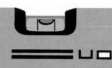

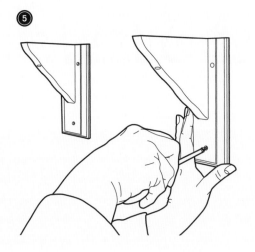

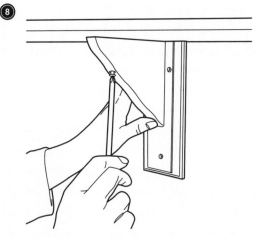

WHAT TO DO

① Choose position for the shelf. If attaching to a stud wall, ensure that the screw positions align with studs. Use a multipurpose detector to locate studs and also to ensure that you're not drilling into any cables or pipes. Generally, it's never a good idea to drill directly above or below light fittings or power outlets.

② Hold shelf in place and mark position of bottom edge on wall in pencil. Use tape measure to mark position of both brackets; make sure they're evenly spaced.

③ Use standard level to check that the shelf line and bracket marks are level.

④ Hold brackets in position and mark position of screw holes on wall with scratch awl or nail.

⑤ Drill holes at markings to depth of wall anchors, if using, and push into hole. For long screws, drill pilot holes. Screw brackets into place.

⑥ Lay shelf on brackets and mark screw holes with scratch awl or nail through bracket on underside of shelf.

⑦ Remove shelf, change drill bit, and drill pilot holes in shelf for screws, if not predrilled. Don't go all the way through the board.

⑧ Put shelf back on brackets and screw into place.

HOW TO NAIL IT!

- Check the orientation of your bracket; the longest arm goes against the wall and the shortest under the shelf.

- If shelves sag, it means the load is too heavy or the shelf is too thin. Move brackets closer together, or turn sagging shelf upside down and add another bracket.

BUILD ALCOVE SHELVES

Alcoves are good places for installing shelves because you get built-in stops and can achieve a really neat, practical finish without too much effort.

▶ YOU'LL NEED

STEEL TAPE MEASURE

PENCIL

TOOL UP JIGSAW
OR CIRCULAR SAW

TOOL DOWN HAND SAW

WORKBENCH OR OTHER SUITABLE CUTTING SURFACE (SEE PAGE 22)

2 X 1-INCH WOODEN BATTENS, LENGTH AS REQUIRED

TIMBER OR ¾-INCH MDF, FOR SHELVES

MULTIPURPOSE DETECTOR

STANDARD LEVEL

⚠ POWER DRILL, WITH COUNTERSINK, AND SUITABLE BITS

SCRATCH AWL OR NAIL

WALL ANCHORS, IF NEEDED

LONG SCREWS, TO GO THROUGH BATTENS AND 1 INCH INTO WALL

SHORT SCREWS, FOR SHELVES

WOOD FILLER

PAINTER'S CAULK AND CAULK GUN

PRIMER, PAINT, AND PAINTBRUSH

GETTING STARTED

Measure width and depth of the alcoves. Using saw, cut a batten to fit back wall and two side battens to fit the depth. Remember to subtract the width of the back batten when cutting the two side battens.

Measure width of alcove at back and front and use narrowest measurement to saw timber or MDF for shelves.

Use a detector to note positions of hidden pipes and cables and avoid attaching there. If not drilling into masonry, locate studs using a detector and attach to these, if possible.

See *Back to Basics* (pages 18–23) for more advice on choosing screws, wall anchors, and drill bits to match your wall, and for tips on sawing and drilling.

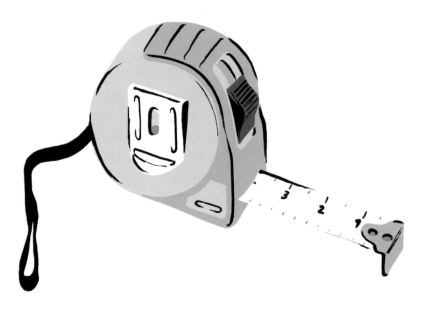

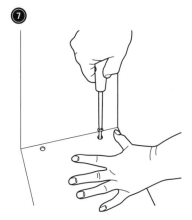

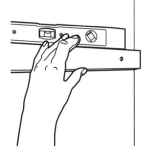

WHAT TO DO

1 Hold standard level against wall and draw pencil line around alcove, where base of each shelf will sit.

2 Drill and countersink holes through center line of each batten (see page 18). Space holes roughly 12 inches apart, at most.

3 Hold rear batten in position with upper edge against pencil line (check again with standard level). Using scratch awl or nail, mark wall through all batten screw holes.

4 Remove batten. Switch to suitable bit. Drill holes to depth of wall anchor, if using, and insert. If attaching to studs, drill pilot holes. Line up batten and attach the screws.

5 Position side battens with upper edge against pencil line and in line with rear batten. Fix side battens in same way, ensuring that they are level. Follow same method for further shelves. Tighten all screws.

6 Drill and countersink screw holes at each corner of shelf where it meets battens.

7 Fix shelf to battens with wood screws. Fill holes with wood filler.

8 Most alcoves will not be "true" (i.e. straight), so hide any gaps at sides with painter's caulk (see page 133). Alternatively, make a template of the shape first with a piece of cardboard.

9 Prime and paint as required. See *Paint Interior Woodwork* (page 168).

HOW TO NAIL IT!

- Think about the height of the items you want to store on your shelves before marking out height of each shelf. Don't forget to take into account the thickness of the shelving material itself.

- For a neat finish, cut the visible ends of the side battens at an angle rather than square, with the longest edge supporting the shelf, so that the battens appear to recede.

- For an even better appearance you can add battens along the front edge and a thin sheet of timber or plyboard on the underside, to cover the batten. This will give it the appearance of a floating shelf.

BUILD SIMPLE ALCOVE CUPBOARDS

Complement your alcove shelving with a cupboard in the lower part of the alcove—a great way of maximizing storage space and clearing things away. This straightforward method is ideal if you are building alcove cupboards for the first time, but it's not necessarily one an experienced carpenter would use!

▶ YOU'LL NEED

TIMBER OR ¾ INCH MDF

MULTIPURPOSE DETECTOR

STANDARD LEVEL, PENCIL

SCRAPER PLUS PRY BAR OR CROWBAR, IF REMOVING BASEBOARDS

STEEL TAPE MEASURE

TOOL UP JIGSAW OR CIRCULAR SAW

TOOL DOWN HAND SAW

WORKBENCH OR OTHER SUITABLE CUTTING SURFACE (SEE PAGE 22)

50 X 1 INCH WOODEN BATTENS, LENGTH AS REQUIRED

⚠ POWER DRILL, WITH COUNTERSINK AND SUITABLE BITS

SCRATCH AWL OR NAIL

WALL ANCHORS, IF NEEDED

LONG SCREWS, TO GO THROUGH BATTENS AND 1 INCH INTO WALL

SHORT SCREWS, FOR SHELVES AND CUPBOARD TOP

SCREWDRIVER, MALLET

6 FLAT METAL ANGLE CORNER BRACES, WITH SCREWS

4 HINGES, WITH SCREWS

PAINTER'S CAULK, WOOD FILLER

PRIMER, PAINT, AND PAINTBRUSHES

SUITABLE HARDWARE

GETTING STARTED

See *Install Simple Shelves* (page 174) for help on which timber to use.

Choose the height of your cupboard. A reasonable guide is just above hip level.

Use a multipurpose detector to note positions of hidden pipes and cables and avoid drilling there. If not drilling into masonry, locate studs using a detector and attach to these, if possible.

See Back to Basics (pages 18-23) for more advice on choosing screws, wall anchors, and drill bits to match your wall, and for tips on sawing and drilling.

⑧　　　　　⑩　　　　　⑮

WHAT TO DO

❶ Use pencil and standard level to draw a line around alcove 2¾ inches below chosen height (to allow for batten and shelf).

❷ Remove baseboard. Gently tap scraper down the back of the top of the boards to break the bond with the paint or any filler. Insert pry bar or crowbar and prize carefully along length of baseboards.

❸ Begin by building a frame. Measure from floor to pencil line at both front edges of alcove. Saw two vertical battens to length.

❹ Attach two vertical battens flush to front of alcove, at either side, with widest part (measuring 2 inches) flat to wall, following method for *Build Alcove Shelves* (page 176).

❺ Measure, cut, and attach top rear horizontal batten and two smaller side battens, as if building a shelf. Align bottom edge of battens with pencil line. Ensure that the side battens fit firmly to top of vertical battens just attached.

❻ Cut and attach battens for any additional shelving inside cupboard, following method for *Build Alcove Shelves* (page 176).

❼ Measure distance between two front vertical battens and cut two horizontal battens to fit snugly between them, one at the top and one at the bottom, running along the floor. Tap gently in place with mallet and check with standard level.

❽ Secure front horizontal battens to vertical battens by screwing in four metal angle corner braces at back of battens, inside cupboard. These screw straight in without predrilling, but drill pilot holes if it's easier.

❾ Measure height from bottom horizontal batten to top. Cut one vertical batten to fit snugly between them.

❿ Measure center point of front horizontal battens and tap vertical batten into place with mallet. Secure as before with two metal angle corner braces.

⓫ Cut and attach any shelves to their battens following method for *Build Alcove Shelves* (page 176). Work from lower shelves upwards.

⓬ Cut cupboard top to size (make it slightly deeper if you want a small lip). Slip cupboard top onto battens. Drill, countersink, and attach screws at each corner, where the top meets the battens. If you feel confident, drill from the inside so you won't get any visible holes.

⓭ Measure area for doors, allowing at least ⅜-inch gap all the way round at each side to allow for doors to open easily. Cut timber or MDF to size.

⓮ Hold doors in position and mark hinge positions on frame and door in pencil. Measure carefully to ensure the same positioning on each door.

⓯ Screw hinges to door inside or outside as preferred; hold in position and screw other half of hinges to frame. Repeat for second door.

⓰ Hide any gaps at sides with painter's caulk (see page 133) and fill all countersunk screw holes with wood filler.

⓱ Sand, prime, and paint cupboard. See *Paint Interior Woodwork* (page 168).

⓲ Add handles and cabinet latches, following manufacturer's instructions.

HOW TO NAIL IT!

- If you feel confident enough, try building the front "frame" of the cupboards flat on the floor, adding the doors, then lifting and securing the whole thing onto the wall at one time.

- If it's not appropriate to take off the baseboards, use slightly wider battens on the front vertical side of the frame and use a jigsaw to cut the shape of the baseboards out of the batten so that it fits snugly.

- Stick a frame of thin MDF strips to the cupboard doors to create a Shaker-style look.

BUILD RTA FURNITURE

Whether you come from the school of thought that believes in following instructions to the letter, or whether you prefer to dive straight in, building ready-to-assemble, or RTA, furniture can be very frustrating indeed. Follow a few simple guidelines and you'll find putting together any type of RTA furniture a little easier.

▶ YOU'LL NEED

RTA FURNITURE PACK (THIS SHOULD CONTAIN EVERYTHING YOU NEED, INCLUDING TOOLS)

BOWLS OR CONTAINERS, FOR SMALL PARTS

A HELPER, IF ASSEMBLING LARGE ITEM

⚠ **POWER DRILL, SCREWDRIVER AND HEX KEY, IF NEEDED**

GETTING STARTED

Clear a large space near where you would like your furniture to be positioned. Unpack the box carefully and lay out all components, including any hardware. Use small pot or bowl for each bag of small parts or screws.

WHAT TO DO

1 Lay furniture panels on a soft surface to prevent scratches.

2 Identify all parts, using the instructions. Make sure you have the right number of everything, checking in the box that nothing has been overlooked. If something is missing, return the complete pack and get a replacement.

3 Build tall pieces on their backs to make assembly easier. If the unit has wheels or casters, fit these last.

4 In general, you will begin with the base panel, then connect side panels. Simple units have predrilled holes and hardware that screw in easily.

5 If your unit has glued dowels and barrel nut or cam lock connectors, place dowels and screwed pegs in base, add glue then push on side panel and tighten barrel nut/cam lock connector. Continue with all panels.

6 Cover discs are sometimes supplied. Use these to cover screw heads and neaten the finish.

7 If you need to add doors, they will be hung on hinges. These hinges fit into predrilled holes on doors and cabinet sides. Fit hinge body to door and mounting plate to cabinet side. Attach with screws provided and adjust until doors hang squarely.

8 Add any shelves and door handles. Make sure all hardware pieces are tight.

9 Fit wheels or casters if needed.

HOW TO NAIL IT!

- Try to be calm and methodical. Estimate the time you think the job will take, then double it. Don't put yourself under time pressure.

- If the unit comes with a hex key, tape this and the instructions to the back of the furniture when complete. This way you can easily dismantle it for moving or selling at a later date.

- Have a basic toolbox on hand. Sometimes the tools provided can be a little flimsy, and you may need to use a power drill, screwdriver, or sturdier hex key.

STRIP PAINTED FURNITURE

If you have a piece of wooden furniture covered in paint or varnish that you've grown tired of, strip it down and rekindle your love for it.

YOU'LL NEED

DROP CLOTH, NEWSPAPER OR OLD CLOTH

SCREWDRIVER, IF NEEDED

PROTECTIVE GLOVES, SAFETY GOGGLES/GLASSES, AND RESPIRATOR MASK

PAINTBRUSH

⚠ **PAINT STRIPPER**

SCRAPER, OLD SPATULA, OR PUTTY KNIFE

OLD TOOTHBRUSH OR COTTON SWABS

CLEAN RAGS

⚠ **MINERAL SPIRITS**

GETTING STARTED

First make sure there's no chance that this is an antique that you might be about to devalue with your improvements.

Work outside if you can. Otherwise, find a well-ventilated place to do your work, with no naked flames nearby.

Note: this method will only work if the bottom coat of paint is oil-based: in other words, old gloss paint. For furniture painted with flat latex, try either sanding or repainting and ageing (see page 182).

⚠ STAY SAFE!

Don't attempt this without wearing protective gloves, goggles, and a respirator mask. Paint stripper really will hurt if it gets on your skin. It can even melt through plastic. If paint stripper does get on your skin, wash it off immediately with soap and warm water.

WHAT TO DO

❶ Lay down drop cloth, newspaper, or old cloth. Set furniture on top.

❷ Using a screwdriver, if necessary, remove any handles or non-wood pieces.

❸ Wearing gloves, safety goggles, and mask, paint thick layer of stripper all over furniture. Leave for 5–10 minutes to work.

❹ Using a scraper, carefully remove the bubbled paint. Don't gouge too deeply.

❺ Use old toothbrush or cotton swabs to work into thin crevices.

❻ Repeat steps 3–5 if the paint is thick or stubborn.

❼ Use clean rags and mineral spirits to wipe down the whole piece. Check manufacturer's advice for guidance on disposal of brushes and chemicals.

HOW TO NAIL IT!

- Pastes and gels can be useful on vertical surfaces since they're less likely to run and drip.
- Don't skimp on the mineral spirits at the final stage.
- Read manufacturer's instructions carefully before using stripper.

PAINT AND AGE FURNITURE

You can give painted furniture an aged or "shabby-chic" look with a few simple techniques that don't involve leaving it out in the rain overnight. These methods are also a good way of covering up scratches or damage without forking out for expensive refinishing.

YOU'LL NEED

DROP CLOTH, NEWSPAPER OR OLD CLOTH

SCREWDRIVER, IF NEEDED

RESPIRATOR MASK

VERY FINE-GRADE SANDPAPER

TOOL UP POWER SANDER

TOOL DOWN SANDING BLOCK

ALL-PURPOSE CLEANER; OR 1 CUP WARM WATER, PLUS ½ CUP VINEGAR, PLUS ¼ TSP DISHWASHING LIQUID

SPONGE OR SOFT CLOTH

MATTE LATEX PAINT

GOOD-QUALITY PAINTBRUSHES

FOR DISTRESSED/AGED FINISH:

FINE-GRADE SANDPAPER

FOR CRACKLE GLAZE:

CRACKLE GLAZE

MATTE LATEX PAINT (NOT NON-DRIP) IN TWO COLORS

GETTING STARTED

Choose how you would like to age your furniture.

Distressed/aged finish: repainting and sanding off the exposed areas that would most likely be worn with age is a simple and effective way to age furniture.

Crackle glaze: a paint-on glaze that causes the topcoat to open in cracks, revealing the paint layer or wood underneath, mimicking old, cracked, porcelain glaze. Choose matte latex paint colors for bottom and topcoat. The topcoat will be the main color of the piece and the bottom coat will show through any distressed areas. Generally, it is a good idea to choose contrasting paint colors.

Work outside if you can. Otherwise, find a well-ventilated place to do your work, with no naked flames nearby.

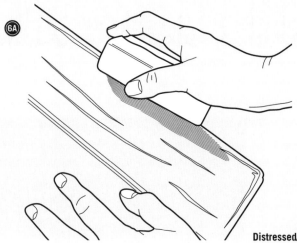

Distressed/aged finish

WHAT TO DO

1 Lay down drop cloth, newspaper, or old cloths. Set furniture on top.

2 Remove any handles or hardware.

3 Wearing a respirator dust mask, prepare all surfaces of furniture by sanding with medium- or fine-grade sandpaper, using power sander or sanding block.

4 Wash down all surfaces with an all-purpose cleaner, or solution of vinegar and detergent.

5 Paint bottom coat of latex all over furniture.

6 A Distressed/aged finish

Paint second coat if needed. Once dry, sand off the piece with fine-grade sandpaper, concentrating on exposed areas—corners, edges, details—rather than large, flat areas.

B Crackle glaze

Paint crackle glaze all over furniture. Apply against grain of wood.

Allow to dry. Paint topcoat in contrasting color over all surfaces, in different direction from glaze. Make sure that the topcoat is of same consistency as light cream. Add water, if needed.

HOW TO NAIL IT!

- For crackle glaze, use a hairdryer to speed up drying and cracking of topcoat.

- Use crackle glaze randomly over large areas to give a more authentic look.

- When distressing furniture, try not to sand off the edges in a uniform line—leave areas where you don't sand so heavily and apply contrasting pressure.

STAIN AND VARNISH FURNITURE

Varnish gives protection against water, dirt, and grease while allowing the natural color of the wood to shine through. If the piece of furniture you're working with is in good condition, staining and varnishing is a great way of showing it off. If the wood's in bad condition, painting may be a better option. See *Paint Interior Woodwork* (page 168), and *Paint and Age Furniture* (page 182).

YOU'LL NEED

STAIN

VARNISH

DROP CLOTH, NEWSPAPER, OR OLD CLOTHS

SCREWDRIVER, IF NEEDED

⚠ PAINT STRIPPER OR FURNITURE REFINISHER, IF NEEDED

PROTECTIVE GLOVES, SAFETY GOGGLES, AND RESPIRATOR MASK, IF USING STRIPPER

PAINTBRUSHES

FINE- AND VERY FINE-GRADE SANDPAPER

🔼 **TOOL UP** POWER SANDER

🔽 **TOOL DOWN** SANDING BLOCK

DAMP CLOTH

RUBBER GLOVES

SEVERAL CLEAN, LINT-FREE CLOTHS AND RAGS

CLEAN CONTAINER

⚠ MINERAL SPIRITS

GETTING STARTED

You can varnish your woodwork without staining it first if you like its natural color, but if you want to enhance the color with stain, you'll need to finish with varnish to give it a protective coat.

Choose stain color and varnish finish. Some varnishes tend to yellow with age, so do your research carefully.

Check tins for guidance on coverage when deciding how much to buy.

Before you begin, make sure the room is well ventilated and warm. If the weather is fine and not windy, work outside.

⚠ STAY SAFE!

Check manufacturer's instructions before disposing of used rags—they can be combustible.

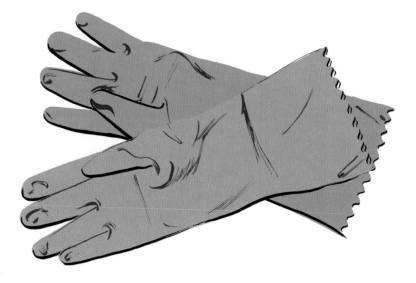

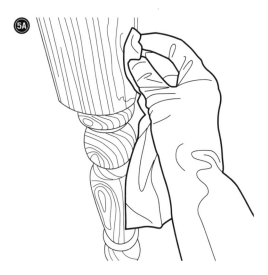

WHAT TO DO

1 Lay down drop cloth, newspaper, or old cloth. Set furniture on top.

2 Using a screwdriver, if necessary, remove any handles or non-wood pieces.

3 If your wood was previously varnished, remove it with furniture refinisher. Follow manufacturer's instructions and wear protective gloves, goggles, and respirator mask. See *Strip Painted Furniture* (page 181).

4 Sand down with fine-grade sandpaper, using power sander or sanding block. Wipe down with damp cloth.

5 **Stain wood**

A Dampen wood first with clean paintbrush. This helps it absorb stain: important for dark colors. Wearing rubber gloves, shake can gently, dip cloth into stain, and apply liberally to wood, along the grain.

B Wipe with a dry cloth to remove excess and get even distribution. Don't leave stain on wood too long. Wipe in direction stain was applied. If stain gets tacky before you wipe it off, apply more stain again, then wipe.

C Leave for one to two hours to dry.

6 **Varnish wood**

A Wearing rubber gloves, mix a diluted varnish in separate, clean container: one part varnish to one part mineral spirits.

B Paint coat of diluted varnish evenly along the grain of wood to seal it. Leave to dry overnight.

C Sand down dry surface with very fine-grade sandpaper, using power sander or sanding block. Wipe down with damp cloth.

D Repeat steps B and C.

E Apply coat of undiluted varnish and leave overnight to dry.

- A handheld power sander or sanding block and sandpaper work well for most wood, but it's easier to get inside small areas and cracks with folded sheets of sandpaper.

- Use 100 percent cotton rags for applying stain. Synthetic fibers may not absorb the stain properly or may leave dyes behind on wood.

- Ideally, use a new brush for applying varnish—or, at least, a very clean one. Also, always pour varnish into a new container; dipping your brush into the can can contaminate it.

HEATING AND INSULATION

EVERYTHING YOU NEED TO GET THE JOB DONE

BLEED HOT-WATER RADIATOR

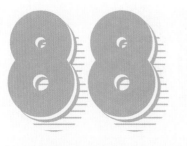

If the top of your hot water radiator is cold while the bottom is warm, it's working inefficiently because there is air in the system. You will need to take the air out of the radiator. This is called "bleeding." If you can't find your radiator vent key, you may be able to find a replacement from a hardware store, or try using a slotted screwdriver instead.

YOU'LL NEED

TOOL UP RADIATOR VENT KEY
TOOL DOWN SLOTTED SCREWDRIVER OR ADJUSTABLE WRENCH
RAG OR SMALL BOWL
CLOTH

GETTING STARTED

First, turn off the central heating.

Start with the highest radiators in your house and work down.

Locate your radiator vent key and the bleed valve, which will be in one of the top corners of the radiator. Some radiators may have a valve that can be turned on with an adjustable wrench.

WHAT TO DO

1 Place a rag or small bowl on the floor underneath valve to protect floor from water spills.

2 Wrap your hands in a cloth.

3 Insert radiator key into valve and turn counterclockwise by a quarter- or half-turn. Do not unscrew by more than one full turn.

4 Listen as the air hisses and escapes. As soon as water starts to appear, turn the key clockwise to shut off the valve.

HOW TO NAIL IT!

• Protect your hands if you are bleeding warm or recently warm radiators; the water splashes could be very hot.

• If your radiators regularly need bleeding, call a heating engineer—there could be a fault in the system.

INSULATE WATER TANKS

All hot water cylinders now come pre-insulated, but if you have an old one that isn't, make insulating it a priority. Cold water tanks also benefit from insulation. Never insulate directly under them, though, because the heat that rises through the ceiling helps to prevent the water from freezing.

▶ YOU'LL NEED

CRAWL BOARD, IF NEEDED
PLUS, AS NEEDED:
HOT OR COLD WATER TANK JACKET
BLANKET INSULATION, PLUS STRING
PROTECTIVE GLOVES AND MASK, IF USING FIBERGLASS
POLYSTYRENE SHEETS
UTILITY KNIFE
DUCT TAPE AND INSULATING TAPE

GETTING STARTED

Make sure you can get to the water tank safely. If it's in your attic and the floor has not been boarded, use a crawl board to work in the area safely.

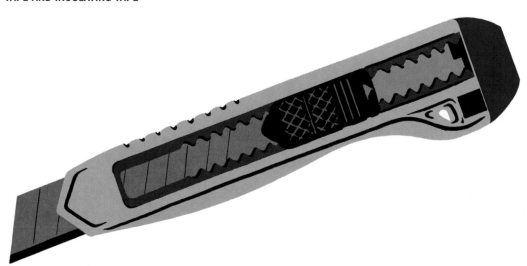

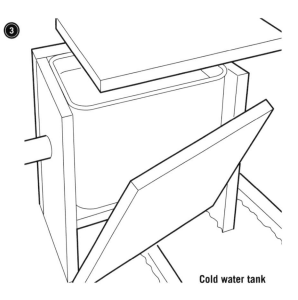

Cold water tank

WHAT TO DO

Cold water tank

1 *Purpose-made jacket:* measure the tank height and width and buy appropriate size. It doesn't matter if it's slightly large, as sections can be overlapped. Refer to manufacturer's instructions.

2 *Blanket insulation:* wear protective gloves and mask, if using fiberglass. Run insulation up four sides of the tank and secure with string. Insulate top with a polystyrene sheet, cut to size. Remember not to insulate directly under the tank.

3 *Polystyrene sheets:* cut to size using utility knife so one sheet lies on top of tank and four run down the sides, extending all the way to the floor. Cut notches from vertical sheets, if needed, for pipes to run through. Secure sheets with duct tape. Seal gaps with insulating tape.

Hot water cylinder

1 To fit purpose-made jacket, unwrap compressed segments so they can expand to full thickness. Loosely tie one strap around cylinder, just below curved top.

2 Working one insulation segment at a time, pull segment up through strap (loosening if necessary) until all are roughly in place.

3 Gather tops of all segments together and thread cord through eyelets. Secure around water outlet pipe. Secure remaining straps around cylinder.

HOW TO NAIL IT!

- If you're going to be insulating your attic floor (see *Insulate Attic*, page 197), plan to insulate your cold water tank at the same time, using the same materials (see *Cold water tank*, step 2).

- It won't be as effective, but if you have old duvets, insulating cylinders and tanks with these is better than nothing!

INSULATE PIPES

Insulating pipes isn't only a matter of saving heat and money. It will also prevent water from freezing in them during the winter, which can end in burst pipes and untold damage. It's important to insulate pipes anywhere they run through unheated spaces.

▶ YOU'LL NEED

UTILITY KNIFE

TUBULAR PIPE INSULATION, SUITABLE LENGTH AND DIAMETER FOR EXPOSED PIPES

CABLE TIES

DUCT TAPE

⚠ JUNIOR HACKSAW

WORKBENCH OR OTHER SUITABLE CUTTING SURFACE (SEE PAGE 22)

GETTING STARTED

Make sure you can access the pipes safely. Cut away any old or degraded insulation with a utility knife and dispose of it.

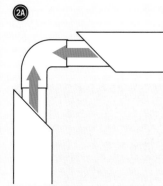 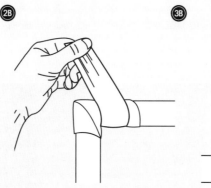 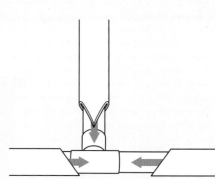

Insulate right-angled joints

Insulate T-joints

WHAT TO DO

❶ Open tubular pipe insulation along slit and slip onto pipe. Secure with cable ties and duct tape around joints.

❷ Insulate right-angled joints

A Cut 45-degree angles with junior hacksaw. You can do this by sight. Since the insulation is soft and joints are taped together, angles can be approximate.

B Push cut edges together and secure with duct tape.

❸ Insulate T-joints

A Cut the ends of the insulation for the two "arms" of the joint with opposite miters, so that when slotted onto the pipe they leave an arrow shape between them.

B Cut a corresponding arrow shape out of the insulation for the third pipe, which should fit snugly between. Secure with duct tape.

❹ Insulate obstructions

To fit around faucets and other obstructions, slit along center of insulation opposite pre-made slit, so that the insulation forms two flaps to wrap around obstruction. Secure with duct tape.

HOW TO NAIL IT!

- Buy the most expensive insulation you can afford and do not be tempted to use pipe tapes, which will degrade.

- If using tie wraps to secure your insulation, don't tie them so tightly that they press into it.

- You could use a miter block and saw if you'd like to make really precise angles.

FIX NOISY PIPES

91

Pipes can make a noise when water flows through them for a number of reasons. The first step is to identify the cause. After that, the remedies are simple.

▶ YOU'LL NEED

SCREWDRIVER

BUFFERS, SUCH AS FOAM INSULATION, RUBBER, KITCHEN SPONGE PIECES, OR OLD GARDEN HOSE

SCREWS AND WALL ANCHORS, IF NEEDED

GETTING STARTED

First, find the location of the noisy pipes, then follow the checks, below, to help you find the source of the noise.

- To check for loose pipes, turn on cold water and see if the pipe(s) are moving at the site of the noise. The pipe may be moving within its clasp, against a wall, or two pipes may be banging together.

- If there is no movement, turn on hot water only. If knocking happens, it could be steam from water that's too hot running through system.

- If pipe makes noise from hot and cold water, but it's securely fixed, the pipe could be too small to cope with water supply, or be compromised (partly blocked) by mineral deposits.

- If you hear a hammering sound when you turn off a running tap, the air chambers in the plumbing system may have become waterlogged.

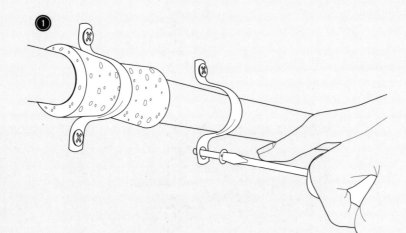

WHAT TO DO

① Fix loose pipes: if the clasps attaching the pipes to the wall have become loose, fasten screws, or cushion pipe movement by filling the clasp space with foam insulation, rubber, sponge, or old hose. If two pipes are banging together, put insulation between them. You may need to replace the original screws with longer ones, or replace wall anchors.

② Fix steam knocking: turn down water heater temperature. Also refer to manufacturer's instructions to try and reduce water pressure in system.

③ Fix compromised pipes: replace pipe. This is a job best left to a plumber or, for a temporary fix, insulate the pipe (see page 190) to dampen the noise.

④ Fix hammering water pipes: turn off water supply. Turn on all faucets in the house and wait until water has completely drained from system. Turn off faucets and turn on the water again, and the air chambers should fill with air.

HOW TO NAIL IT!

• If the noises persist, call a plumber, who should be able to fix the problem easily.

• When tightening pipe fastenings, always leave some room for the pipes to expand and contract with the temperature. Any cushioning you use should have some give.

WEATHERPROOF DOOR

92

Draughty doors are fine when you want to let in fresh air during the summer, but in colder months you are wasting heat by allowing it to escape through gaps. Simple adjustments can help keep the heat in and save you money.

REUSABLE TACK PUTTY

DAMP CLOTH

STEEL TAPE MEASURE

SELF-ADHESIVE FOAM WEATHERSTRIP, AT SIZE REQUIRED FOR GAPS

SCISSORS

FINISH NAILS (OPTIONAL)

GETTING STARTED

Find out how big the gaps in the door frame are by opening the door, pushing tack putty into the space between the frame and the door at one of the edges, then closing the door. Carefully remove the tack and measure the width it has squished to. Repeat for each frame edge, apart from door stop, in case gaps vary in size. Use these measurements as a guide for the size of foam strip needed.

WHAT TO DO

1 Clean dirt and loose paint from the doorframe with a damp cloth. Leave to dry.

2 Measure foam strip against doorframe and cut to size.

3 Remove backing paper and apply along the top and two sides of doorframe.

4 To hold foam strip in place more securely, use a small finish nail at each end.

HOW TO NAIL IT!

- Add keyhole and mail-slot covers, if needed, to your external doors to stop draughts coming through these holes, too.

- Screw a draught-excluding door sweep to the bottom edge of external doors.

WEATHERPROOF WINDOW

If you have draughty old windows, you may be fighting a losing battle to keep the warm air inside. Of course, curtains are a great insulator, but there is more you can do. Try fitting foam weatherstripping or a weatherstripping brush seal. Some brush seals are self-adhesive, but using finish nails holds them securely.

▶ YOU'LL NEED

REUSABLE TACK PUTTY

STEEL TAPE MEASURE

DAMP CLOTH

SELF-ADHESIVE FOAM WEATHERSTRIP, AT SIZE REQUIRED FOR GAPS

SCISSORS

FOR SASH WINDOWS:

STEEL TAPE MEASURE

WEATHERSTRIP SYNTHETIC PILE (BRUSH SEAL), TO FIT UPPER AND LOWER SLIDING EDGES

⚠ **JUNIOR HACKSAW OR STRONG SCISSORS**

WORKBENCH OR OTHER SUITABLE CUTTING SURFACE (SEE PAGE 22)

MASKING TAPE, IF NEEDED

HAMMER

FINISH NAILS

GETTING STARTED

See instructions for *Weatherproof Door* (opposite) to measure gaps in frame edges using reusable tack.

WHAT TO DO

Casement windows

Fit foam weatherstripping to all edges of window frame following instructions for *Weatherproof Door* (opposite).

Sash windows

❶ Fit foam weatherstripping to the top and bottom (non-sliding) edges of window frame (see opposite).

❷ Measure length of each sash and cut brush seal at a 90-degree angle with hacksaw or scissors, to fit.

❸ Position brush seal on inside frame alongside length of lower sash, holding it in place with masking tape, if necessary. Hammer finish nails through predrilled holes to secure seal to frame. Repeat for other side of lower sash.

❹ Position brush seal on outside frame alongside length of upper sash, holding it in place with masking tape, if necessary. Hammer finish nails through predrilled holes to secure seal to frame. Repeat for other side of upper sash.

HOW TO NAIL IT!

- You could also install a swing bar lock on casement window to keep window and frames securely pressed together. See *Install Window Locks* (page 208).

❸

INSTALL ATTIC FLOORBOARDS

To use your attic for storage you need to board over the joists; do not place anything between the joists or it may fall through. If you have insulated the attic (see page 198), you'll need to make sure the boards don't compress the insulation too much or they will affect its efficiency. You can buy special vented attic flooring , but these are more expensive than tongue-and-groove particle boards.

YOU'LL NEED

RESPIRATOR MASK, PROTECTIVE GLOVES, AND CLOTHING

KNEEPADS (OPTIONAL)

CRAWL BOARD, BIG ENOUGH TO SPAN FOUR JOISTS

TIMBER AND LONG SCREWS FOR RAISING JOIST HEIGHT, IF NEEDED

STEEL TAPE MEASURE

ATTIC DECKING BOARD OR FLOORING PANELS

TOOL UP JIGSAW OR CIRCULAR SAW
TOOL DOWN HANDSAW

WORKBENCH OR OTHER SUITABLE CUTTING SURFACE (SEE PAGE 22)

POWER DRILL, WITH WOOD BITS

LONG SCREWS

SCREWDRIVER

CHISEL AND MALLET, IF NEEDED

PENCIL

GETTING STARTED

Note that boarded attic floors are often only strong enough for storage, but not generally for habitation. Be aware, too, that joists were only designed to hold up the ceiling below and may not be strong enough to hold lots of heavy storage. Once you've installed boards, keep in mind how much weight they can bear.

To board an attic floor for anything more than light storage, consult a professional.

Make sure you buy attic boards that fit through your attic hatch or doorway.

You can't attach panels to joists if there are any wires or insulation running across them. If this is the case, attach pieces of 3 x 1 inch timber across the joists at 90 degrees, so that you raise the joist height by 1 inch. Raising joists stops insulation from being compressed and aids airflow.

⚠ STAY SAFE!

• Wear protective clothing, gloves, and a respirator mask, particularly if working near fiberglass insulation.

• Stand or kneel on crawl board while doing any work in attic, to avoid slipping between joists and making a hole in your ceiling. Kneepads will make the job more comfortable.

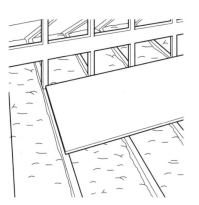

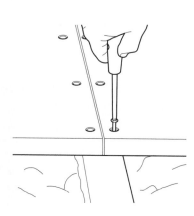

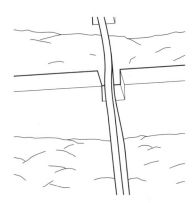

WHAT TO DO

❶ Measure area of boards needed by multiplying width by length of area to be covered. Add a little extra for wastage.

❷ Lay first row of boards out, end to end, at right-angles across joists. Make sure each is across at least three joists. Cut with handsaw, jigsaw, or circular saw to ensure ends reach center of joist.

❸ Butt second board up to first and secure tongue into groove. Using wood bit, drill pilot hole through boards and into joists to depth of screw. If you don't want your screws to stand above the wood, drill countersink holes to sink them lower (see page 18). Secure boards to joist with screws.

❹ Work with one row of boards at a time and for subsequent rows, cut boards as needed so that joins are staggered and don't line up.

❺ At light fixtures, cut holes in board to enable access.

❻ If wires have to run below the boards, you can chisel a notch in the joist for them to run through without being squashed. Mark positions on boards in pencil for future reference.

HOW TO NAIL IT!

- Modern vented attic floorboards allow insulation to "breathe," allow you see any wiring underneath, and come with their own screws. It's worth doing some research to check whether these are suitable for your attic.

- Mark the top of board in pencil if there is anything you are covering over, so that you know which board to lift if you need it in the future.

INSULATE ATTIC

Insulating the attic prevents heat from escaping through your house. You can insulate between or on rafters directly under your roof. Alternatively, you can insulate between or on joists directly above the ceiling of your top floor. If you insulate the rafters, you'll create a warm attic, which can lead to "ice dams" on the roof. If you insulate the attic floor, you'll create a cold attic but keep the heat in the house below.

▶ YOU'LL NEED

FOR FLOOR:
STEEL TAPE MEASURE
⚠ INSULATION, TO COVER FLOOR SPACE, PLUS EXTRA
RECESSED LIGHT COVERS, IF NEEDED
RESPIRATOR MASK, PROTECTIVE GLOVES, AND CLOTHING
KNEEPADS (OPTIONAL)
LAMP OR FLASHLIGHTS, IF NEEDED
⚠ CHISEL OR CROWBAR
CRAWL BOARD, BIG ENOUGH TO SPAN FOUR JOISTS
2 PIECES OF SCRAP WOOD
UTILITY KNIFE
MATERIAL TO INSULATE PIPES AND ATTIC HATCH, IF NECESSARY
FOR RAFTERS:
⚠ INSULATION, TO COVER SPACE, PLUS EXTRA (SEE *GETTING STARTED*)
STAPLE GUN
TAPE, IF USING SOFT INSULATION
TO EXTEND RAFTER DEPTH:
BATTENS, AS REQUIRED FOR HEIGHT NEEDED
⚠ POWER DRILL, WITH WOOD BITS
LONG SCREWS

⚠ STAY SAFE!

• Wear protective clothing, gloves, and a respirator mask, particularly if working with fiberglass insulation.

• Laying insulation over electrical cables can be dangerous. Carefully lift them up to lie above the insulation, or tie them to the top of your joists.

• Keep insulation clear of recessed lights. Protect any halogen or spotlights with recessed light covers—conical or cylinder-shaped fire protectors (**A**). Insulation should be at least 3 inches away from recessed light fittings and hot flues.

• If in any doubt about dealing with electrical wires and insulation issues, consult a qualified electrician.

• Stand or kneel on crawl board while doing any work in attic, to avoid slipping between joists and making a hole in your ceiling. Kneepads will make the job more comfortable.

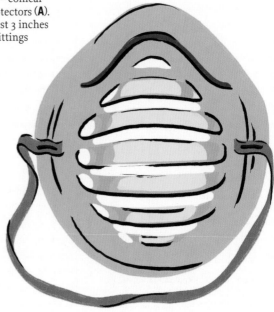

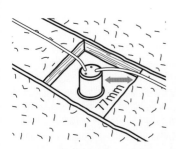

GETTING STARTED

First, choose the insulation material. For attic floors, the material should be between R-30 and R-60, depending on what zone you live in, according to US Department of Energy guidelines; a good rule of thumb, though, is that if your existing insulation isn't up to 19 inches deep, add more to reduce your energy bills. This can be made up from different layers. Remember, though, that cheap insulation is often less dense and less effective than better-quality products.

Blanket insulation: Comes in pre-cut batt or roll form to fit between joists or rafters and is made from mineral fibers, such as fiberglass or rock wool. A skin irritant, so you must wear gloves, protective clothing, and a face mask when installing it. It comes with or without a vapor barrier. The cheapest insulation.

Encapsulated insulation: This is rock wool insulation "encapsulated" in a thin plastic and metallic film so it's easier to handle – although protective gloves and clothing should still be worn.

Rigid insulation: Made from fibrous material or polystyrene or polyurethane foam board, the slabs are semi-rigid so they can be slotted into position between rafters. May have reflective foil surface on one side.

Blown-in or loose-fill insulation: Usually made from cellulose (recycled paper fiber) or fiberglass, and blown into hard-to-reach crawl spaces.

Sheep's wool insulation: Made from 75-85 percent wool, it's non-irritant and easy to install. It is the most expensive type but is an organic and renewable resource and, arguably, the most effective.

Measure space between joists. To reach your ideal insulation depth, you may have to insulate between joists first then with top this with a second layer. If space between joists is full, lay the second layer over top of joists at right angles to them. Check depth of joists before ordering insulation and consider whether you are planning to put floorboards in your attic.

Calculate how many rolls of insulation you'll need for the first layer by multiplying the width of the attic by its length, subtracting 10 percent (for space taken up by joists), and dividing by the area each roll provides. Repeat for top-up layer without taking away 10 percent, as this layer sits on top of and covers joists.

For insulation between rafters, measure the area of roof and subtract 10 percent for rafters.

Before you insulate, use the opportunity to have a good look at your attic space and check for any signs of leaks or condensation. If you find any, contact a local roofer for professional advice.

WHAT TO DO

1 Clear your attic of any stored items. Make sure you have enough light. Rig up a lamp or get good battery-powered flashlights where there is no permanent attic light.

2 Carry as much insulation as you can into attic before starting, to minimize trips up and down ladder.

3 Insulate attic floor

A Remove any attic boards to reveal joists, by prying up with chisel or crowbar. Place crawl board across timber near the eaves to work from. Move board across floor to support you as you go.

B Check manufacturer's instructions for right-side up. Starting at eaves, unroll insulation along gap. If you have a non-breathable roof, leave a 2-inch gap where the roof rafters meet the floor joists. Press insulation down for snug fit. Avoid leaving gaps—the heat will find them.

C When one length has been filled, compress insulation between pieces of scrap wood, then cut with knife or scissors. Cut insulation at crossbeams, then unroll from opposite eaves towards beam.

D Roll out second, top-up layer at right angles to first until floor covered. Insulate cold water tank, if present (see page 188).

E Insulate exposed pipes (see page 190).

INSULATE ATTIC

⑤

F Insulate the attic hatch using a special attic-hatch insulator (available from large hardware stores). Alternatively, fill a large bag with insulating material and staple it down, or glue a block of slab insulation in place.

❹ Insulate between rafters using slabs

A Check rafters will allow for the insulation depth. Extend rafter depth, if necessary, by screwing on battens.

B Starting from top and working down, one rafter at a time, fit slabs between rafters. If they need cutting, leave them slightly oversized so they'll fit by friction.

❺ Insulate rafters using soft insulation

This is an alternative to insulating between rafters. Working horizontally, staple insulation to rafters, butting sheets together. Secure with tape.

HOW TO NAIL IT!

- **The US Department of Energy recommends different R-values for different parts of the country. If you have old insulation that has compressed to less than this, top it up with other material to the minimum thickness. Any pre-existing insulation of less than 4 inches is worth getting rid of so you can start again.**

- **Do not insulate directly over recessed light fixtures unless they have the appropriate safety rating.**

- **Always check to see whether or not you need a vapor barrier or retarder. Some insulation comes with a vapor barrier on one side. If you're topping up only, check beneath the existing insulation to see if a vapor barrier is in place.**

HOME SAFETY AND SECURITY

EVERYTHING YOU NEED TO GET THE JOB DONE

INSTALL SMOKE DETECTORS

Having working detectors in your home can be a literal lifesaver: You are twice as likely to die in a house fire if you have none. Fumes from a smoldering fire can build up overnight as you sleep, so a smoke alarm may be your first and only warning.

▶ YOU'LL NEED

SMOKE OR CARBON-MONOXIDE DETECTORS, WITH HARDWARE

MULTIPURPOSE DETECTOR, IF NEEDED

BATTERIES, IF NEEDED

SCRATCH AWL OR NAIL

⚠ **POWER DRILL, WITH APPROPRIATE BITS FOR WALL TYPE OR CEILING**

SUITABLE ANCHORS FOR WALL TYPE OR CEILING, IF NEEDED

SCREWDRIVER

GETTING STARTED

Decide which type of detector you need. Be sure to look for one that is UL-listed. Your detector can be battery-operated, hard-wired, or a combination of both. Others simply plug in to existing standard electrical outlets.

Ionization smoke detector: the cheapest to buy. This will go off when it senses small smoke particles from flaming fires, such as from a frying pan or burning food.

Carbon-monoxide detector: essential if you have any appliance that uses gas, oil, wood, or coal. Even water heaters, furnaces, and well-controlled open fires or log burners can be killers. If they aren't burning efficiently or the room isn't well ventilated, they can produce the lethal gas carbon monoxide, which is undetectable until it's too late.

Combined detector: Buy combined smoke and carbon-monoxide detectors and you're covered for both types of danger.

Decide where to position your detectors. In kitchens, the National Fire Protection Association recommends that they be positioned 10 feet away from cooking appliances. Install detectors within 15 feet of sleeping areas so that everyone can hear the alarm if it goes off—even if their doors are closed.

See *Back to Basics* (pages 18-20) for advice on choosing screws, wall anchors, and drill bits to match your wall, and for tips on drilling.

WHERE TO POSITION ALARMS

Ⓐ **Single-story homes:** in hallway, between sleeping and living areas. Ideally place on ceiling, at least 12 inches away from wall or light fixture. On inside walls, place 6-12 inches lower than ceiling height.

Ⓑ **Large or multistory homes:** as above, plus at bottom of staircase and on each staircase landing. Also consider buying interconnected alarms so that smoke or heat detected on one level can trigger alarms all over the house.

Ⓒ **Homes with real fires or natural gas supply:** as above, with additional carbon-monoxide alarm. If you are using a combination smoke alarm, fit as smoke alarm. Otherwise, fit in same room as appliance or somewhere central (hallway, landing), at head height, at least one yard from furnace, fire, or heater and not directly above anything that gives off steam.

WHAT TO DO

❶ Locate best position for alarms (see *Getting Started*). Use a multipurpose detector to find positions of hidden pipes and cables and avoid drilling there. Unless wall is masonry, locate studs using a detector and attach to these, if possible.

❷ Remove cover of alarm and install batteries, if needed, following manufacturer's instructions.

❸ Hold back plate to wall or ceiling and mark screw points with scratch awl or nail through holes. Drill holes to depth of anchors, if using, and push in. If attaching to studs or rafters, drill pilot holes.

❹ Screw the alarm in position. Replace cover and test.

HOW TO NAIL IT!

• Check your alarm batteries regularly and replace any dead batteries immediately (usually after 12 months). Always recycle used batteries.

• If you are worried about losing battery power, you can find alarms that wire into the electricity supply (backed up by batteries).

INSTALL DOOR VIEWER

97

A door viewer is a simple device to fit and gives an added level of security by allowing you to see who is at the door before you decide whether or not to open it.

YOU'LL NEED

STEEL TAPE MEASURE
DOOR VIEWER, WITH HARDWARE
PENCIL, SCRATCH AWL, OR NAIL
⚠ POWER DRILL, WITH SUITABLE BITS
SCREWDRIVER

GETTING STARTED

Measure the thickness of your front door and buy a door viewer to fit; they come in varying sizes.

Choose a height for the door viewer that most members of the household will be able to look through comfortably.

WHAT TO DO

1 Measure the width of the door and find the midpoint at your chosen height. Mark position with a pencil, scratch awl, or nail.

2 Drill hole in door using appropriately sized drill bit. Drill until the bit almost emerges through the door, then drill back in from the other side.

3 Push outside half of door viewer into the door.

4 Screw in inside half on other side of door. Tighten the pieces together by hand and finish with screwdriver.

HOW TO NAIL IT!

- Use a small drill bit to create a small pilot hole before you drill the main hole. This will help you to keep straight and give you confidence.

- To replace a damaged door viewer, use a screwdriver to remove it. Clean any dirt and debris from the hole before installing new door viewer as above.

INSTALL DOOR CHAIN GUARD

Even if you have a door viewer in your front door, you should consider fitting a door chain guard as an extra level of security. If you have a UPVC front door, keep away from glass borders and use self-drilling screws that screw directly into the aluminum inside the door.

YOU'LL NEED

DOOR CHAIN GUARD, WITH HARDWARE
PENCIL, SCRATCH AWL, OR NAIL
STANDARD LEVEL
⚠ POWER DRILL, WITH SUITABLE BITS
SCREWDRIVER
⚠ CHISEL AND MALLET, IF NEEDED

GETTING STARTED

Choose height for your chain and mark screw holes for chain slider on inside of your front door with a pencil, scratch awl, or nail. The usual position would be near the latch for ease of access. Check that the holes are level using standard level.

WHAT TO DO

1 Drill pilot holes at marks using drill bit smaller than the fastening screws. Screw on the chain slider.

2 Mark position of chain holder on door frame. This should align with the chain slider.

3 Mark screw holes for chain holder. Drill pilot holes and screw chain holder in place.

4 Test chain.

HOW TO NAIL IT!

• For a clean finish in a wooden door, recess the chain holder into the door frame. Before screwing it in place, hold chain holder in position and draw round it. Use a chisel and mallet to carve out the recess. Stand in a steady position when working with a chisel and watch your fingers; chisels can be extremely sharp.

INSTALL DOOR LOCKS

99

The more locks on your front door and the more levers or pins a lock has, the more secure your home will be. That said, you don't need to go wild; a mortise lock and a rim cylinder deadbolt night latch are usually fine. If you only want one lock on your door, choose something really secure that you can deadlock.

▶ YOU'LL NEED

STEEL TAPE MEASURE

MORTISE LOCK OR RIM CYLINDER DEADBOLT NIGHT LATCH LOCK SET, WITH HARDWARE

PENCIL AND RULER

⚠ POWER DRILL, WITH WOOD AND SUITABLE BITS, PLUS WIDE WOODCUTTING BIT FOR CYLINDER DEADBOLT

MASKING TAPE

DOOR WEDGE

⚠ WIDE AND NARROW CHISELS

MALLET

⚠ KEYHOLE OR HOLE SAW, FOR SHAPING MORTISE LOCK KEYHOLE

SCRATCH AWL OR NAIL

SCREWDRIVER

⚠ JUNIOR HACKSAW, IF NEEDED

WORKBENCH OR OTHER SUITABLE CUTTING SURFACE, IF NEEDED (SEE PAGE 22)

GETTING STARTED

Measure your door before you buy any locks, to make sure they will fit. This job assumes you will be installing locks in a wooden door.

Choose positions for your locks:

Mortise lock: about halfway up the door where, importantly, the timber is solid. If your door is paneled, avoid the joint of the horizontal rail or you could weaken the door's structure.

Rim cylinder deadbolt night latch: position one-third of way down the door from the top.

Read manufacturer's instructions before starting.

WHAT TO DO

Install mortise lock

❶ Open front door and mark midpoint in pencil on side edge at the required height.

❷ Hold lock edge (deep recessed part) up to the side edge of door and mark top and bottom edges. Draw vertical midpoint line with pencil and ruler.

❸ Select drill bit $1/16$ inch wider than lock body. Mark depth of lock on drill bit with masking tape.

❹ Hold door steady with a door wedge. Drill out lock recess by making series of overlapping holes down along vertical pencil line.

❺ Use chisel and mallet to open up row of circular holes into rectangular shape to fit lock.

❻ Insert lock and draw around faceplate position with pencil.

❼ Using chisel and mallet, cut out recess for faceplate within markings. Start by making a series of cuts on the pencil outline, then chisel out, a little at a time. Keep testing until you have a good fit.

❽ Hold lock body against face of door and mark location of keyhole. Repeat on other side of door.

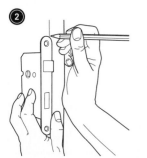

Install mortise lock

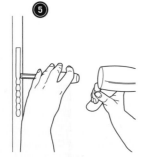

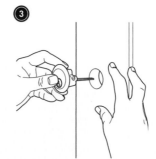

**Install rim cylinder deadbolt
night latch**

(9) Cut out keyhole each side. Shape using wood drill bit slightly larger than keyhole. Use keyhole saw for lower part. Cut out bottom with narrow chisel.

(10) Push in lock and test keys.

(11) Hold faceplate in position, mark fixing positions with scratch awl or nail and screw into place, drilling pilot holes first, if necessary.

(12) Screw on keyhole covers, drilling pilot holes first, if necessary.

(13) With bolt out and held against doorframe, mark strike plate position and depth of bolt box. Use marks to position strike plate on inside surface of doorframe. Use template if provided.

(14) Use chisel and mallet to cut out wood for the hole receiving the bolt. Chisel a little at a time and keep testing for fit.

(15) Check that the door closes properly. Chisel out recess for striking plate as above, testing until you have a good fit. Screw plate into place and test.

Install rim cylinder deadbolt

(1) Mark position of hole for lock cylinder, at comfortable height, about 2 inches in from edge of door.

(2) Check instructions for diameter of hole before selecting your drill bit. Drill hole. When drill bit begins to emerge from other side of door, change sides and complete hole from the other side.

(3) Fit cylinder parts together and insert into hole from outside. The cylinder should have enough room to turn.

(4) Secure mounting plate in position on inside of door using connecting screws so both plate and keyhole remain in the correct upright position.

(5) Place lock case in position on mounting plate. The connecting bar may need shortening. If so, do this with junior hacksaw. If door edge needs cutting to fit lip of lock case, use chisel and mallet. Keep testing for fit as you work.

(6) Mark screw positions and drill pilot holes, if necessary. Fasten lock case to door with screws.

(7) Line up striking plate with bolt and mark its position on door frame with pencil. Use chisel to create recess for striking plate, if required.

(8) Mark fastening positions with scratch awl or nail and screw in securely.

HOW TO NAIL IT!

- **For added security you can fit a bolt 6 inches lower than the top door hinge and 6 inches higher than the bottom hinge.**

- **Many locks come with templates for fitting. Using these will save any measurement errors!**

INSTALL WINDOW LOCKS

100

Block a potentially easy-access point for burglars by installing window locks. Different window types require different locks. Make sure you keep the keys in the same room and know where they are in case of emergencies.

▶ YOU'LL NEED

- **CASEMENT WINDOW LOCK OR SASH WINDOW LOCK, PLUS HARDWARE**
- **STEEL TAPE MEASURE**
- **PENCIL, SCRATCH AWL, OR NAIL**
- **SCREWDRIVER**
- ⚠ **POWER DRILL, WITH WOOD BITS, IF NEEDED**

GETTING STARTED

Choose the type of lock suitable for your windows.

There are a number of options for casement windows. Most locks are made up of two parts that fix to both the frame and window and lock together. You can also buy locking handles and stay locks that can lock a window while slightly open, allowing for ventilation.

For sash windows, you can choose from various types of surface-fitted locks where a clasp is fixed to the upper sash and a receiver to the lower sash. Sash or slide window stops are easy to install, but permanently limit the amount you can open the window. They prevent the lower sash or sliding window from being opened completely.

Install lock on casement window

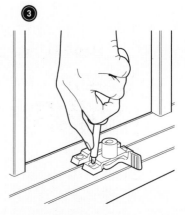

Install lock on sash windows

Install casement window lock

❶ Open window and mark the position of locking plate 1mm from edge of fixed frame.

❷ Mark attachment holes with scratch awl or nail. Screw on locking plate.

❸ Close window. Find the correct position of locking section against the plate and mark position of screw holes with scratch awl or nail.

❹ Loosely attach locking section in position with one screw.

❺ Check that the locking mechanism fits properly and adjust it if necessary.

❻ Screw on locking section securely.

❼ Close window, close the lock, and fasten it securely.

Install sash window lock

❶ With sash windows in closed position, measure to find the center of the rail furthest from you—this is the upper sash. Mark in pencil.

❷ Place lock in position, centered over pencil mark, and mark screw holes with scratch awl or nail. Screw lock on.

❸ Place the receiver part of the lock onto rail of sash closest to you and align it with the lock. Mark screw holes with scratch awl or nail.

❹ Loosely fix receiver part into position with one screw.

❺ Check that the lock works properly and adjust it if necessary.

❻ Screw securely into place.

HOW TO NAIL IT!

- Even if your windows are locked, intruders could be able to smash glass to get into your home. Laminated glass and double glazing help security, but you should still check that the glazing compound and pushpoints or finish nails aren't loose; otherwise the pane could be easily removed.

- Vinyl windows usually come with quality locks; if not, contact the supplier to install them, rather than trying to do the job yourself.

- If you find driving screws directly into the scratch-awl holes difficult, drill small pilot holes first.

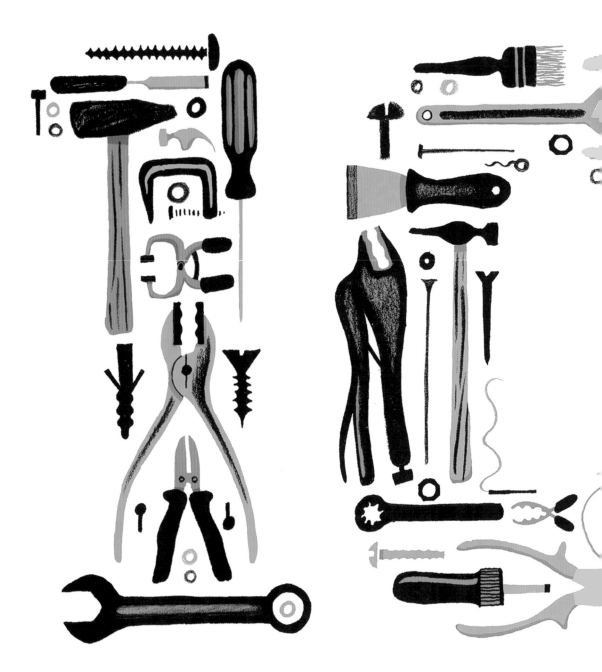

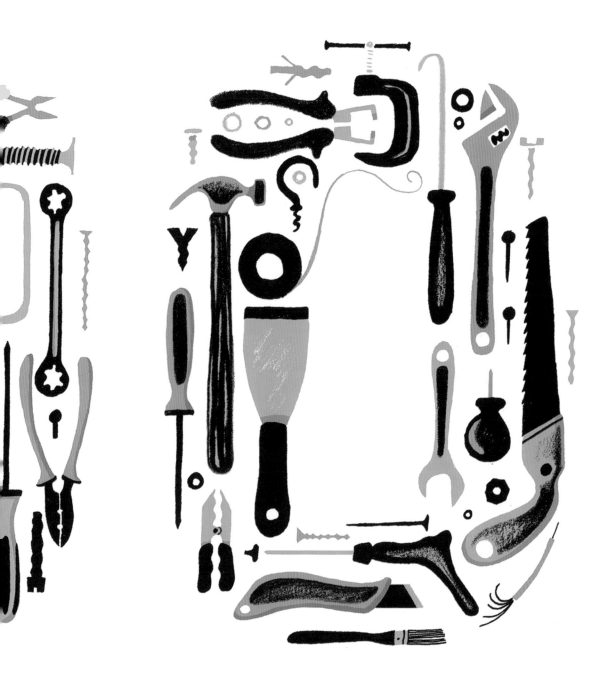

INDEX

FIND
EVERYTHING
YOU NEED
HERE

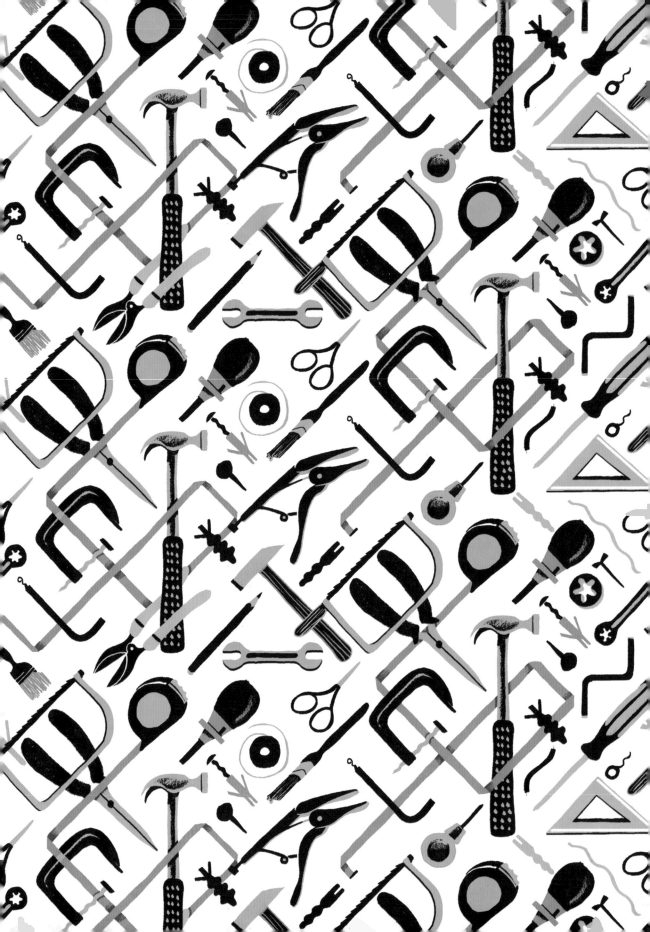

Author's acknowledgments

Thank you to all those at Quadrille Publishing and beyond, to those who helped research and shape the book, and the wonderful designers and illustrators who have achieved the impossible: making a DIY book look utterly gorgeous!

I consider myself incredibly lucky. I'm surrounded by truly great people who, because they do the brilliant jobs they do, have given me the inspiration and the time to write this book.

Thank you to the wonderful team at Rise Hall. I can't tell you the difference you have made. Thank you to the brilliant team at Tepilo, for turning my online real-estate-agency dream into a reality. Thank you to the fabulous MySingleFriend.com team; you are a ray of sunshine in a dark and lonely world! Thank you to Red House TV and Channel 4; you make my job a total joy. Thank you to Paul Stevens, my book agent, and Laura Hill, my agent, for the constant encouragement.

Last, but by no means least, thank you, Graham, for your sound judgment and unfaltering support.